The Christian Entrepreneur

Bridging the gap between our Christian walk, faith, service, ministry, business, success and authentic living.

First published by Busybird Publishing 2017
Copyright © 2017 The Christian Entrepreneur

ISBN
Print: 978-1-925692-20-4
Ebook: 978-1-925692-29-7

The Christian Entrepreneur has asserted her right under the Copyright, Designs and Patents Act 1988 to be identified as the author of this work. The information in this book is based on the author's experiences and opinions. The publisher specifically disclaims responsibility for any adverse consequences, which may result from use of the information contained herein. Permission to use information has been sought by the author. Any breaches will be rectified in further editions of the book.

All rights reserved. No part of this publication may be reproduced, stored in or introduced into a retrieval system, or transmitted in any form, or by any means (electronic, mechanical, photocopying, recording or otherwise) without the prior written permission of the author. Any person who does any unauthorised act in relation to this publication may be liable to criminal prosecution and civil claims for damages. Enquiries should be made through the publisher.

Cover image: Market Me Marketing
Cover design: Market Me Marketing
Layout and typesetting: Busybird Publishing:
Editor: Helen Henry

Busybird Publishing
2/118 Para Road
Montmorency, Victoria
Australia 3094
www.busybird.com.au

This book contains stories contributed by key Christian entrepreneurs across Australia, who have shared their stories, advice and tips for the purpose of encouraging, challenging and empowering Christians, not only in their businesses but also for those wanting to live an authentic life as they serve in their workplaces.

Our contributors share from a variety of backgrounds, experiences and denominations and we know that you the reader will benefit greatly from this.

To get the most out of this book, we suggest you buy yourself a good quality notebook or journal. Write down any points that are relevant to your situation as you read through each chapter. Write down any revelation or challenge that the Holy Spirit brings to you. As you work through the questions at the end of each chapter, write down your answers and mark any prayer points that you need to focus on. This will help you to formulate a plan to see your vision become a reality
… *write the vision, and make it plain upon tables, that he may run that reads it.* Habakkuk 2:2 (NKJ)

Scriptures used in this book are from several different versions of the Bible.

Contents

Introduction	i
PART A – The Christian Entrepreneur	1
Chapter One – Calling, Purpose, Impact, Authentically Aligned	3
PART B – The Christian Entrepreneur	17
Chapter Two – Giving Wings to Magnificent Dreams by Maree Cutler-Naroba	19
Chapter Three – Finding Freedom by Brenda Tsiaousis	37
Chapter Four – What Are You Worth? by Darryl Stringer	55
Chapter Five – Declutter Your Life by Amy Revell	69
Chapter Six – The Salt of The Earth by Linda Chaousis	85
Chapter Seven – Better, not Bigger by Peter Horsfield	95
Chapter Eight – Releasing the Aroma of Christ by Charmayne Chinnery	113
Chapter Nine – Learning from Our Mistakes by David Daddow	123
Chapter Ten – Nothing is Wasted by Nic Henry Jones	137
PART C – The Christian Entrepreneur Final Thoughts	159
Chapter Eleven – When Things Get Tough by Nic Henry Jones	161
About the Authors	172

Introduction

In our time as Christian entrepreneurs, we've come to realise that our best success comes when we align our business or day job with our faith, service and our impact on the world around us. Our day job and God are not separate.

We were born with certain character traits, with natural inclinations to certain things, given particular spiritual gifts, brought up to facilitate and grow certain skill sets, planted in certain locations for different seasons and presented with different opportunities. Many of us had some idea of what we wanted to be when we grew up, we all had different passions and experiences that contributed to what our careers would or wouldn't be.

Each person is a piece of God's greater puzzle. Everyone has a purpose and God brings forth his plans and purposes for you and your sphere of impact and service (ministry), and it just makes sense that when all these are aligned we live a more authentic and successful life, naturally impacting those around us.

It's Time to Have Some New Conversations

We believe it's time to have different conversations, the hard ones some Christians don't want to have, the ones Christians never thought they would have! But these are the conversations that will empower us for greater impact and ministry and enable Christian business owners to be completely and authentically aligned with their purpose in life.

About the Project ...

We saw a need to publish a book that shares the stories of Christian business owners and entrepreneurs, who see a clear link between what they do in business and their calling in life, their ministry and their mission field. 'The Christian Entrepreneur' is the bringing together of testimonies, struggles and victories experienced by a diverse group of Christian business people. The book also contains some food for thought and some practical empowering strategies they have found to work in their business experience.

The Book is About ...

Changing the mindsets and thought processes around the key topics of calling, ministry and mission and their relationship to business. It is about empowering Christian men and women to be their best, to serve God and people right where they are planted, with the skills they have and the character traits that make them stand out. It's about changing the way we approach business, how we do business, our 'whys' and how God's overall plan for our life and impact fits into that.

Some of the Issues Christian Business Owners Struggle with ...

- Feeling guilty about having a desire to be successful and wanting a six figure income. Thinking that church life and business don't really go together. A simple shift in mindset and a greater understanding of the link between the church and our business can really empower people. Why not be salt and light, while you are working and enjoying life.

- Wondering if what we do in business can really be classed as our ministry to the world. Shouldn't we be running a church to be seen as being 'in ministry'?

- Believing that we can't claim to be a successful person because it's seen as being prideful and wrong.

- Being uncertain of how we can serve people through our business and thereby express our ministry.

- Understanding how being a Christian sets us apart from our competitors.

- Recognising what Christians bring to business that others don't?

- Identifying beliefs about wealth. Is it ok to be wealthy? What does scripture say about wealth?

- Discovering how we can be authentic and express the essence of who we are through our business.

- Discerning what we really need from our churches and what they need from us as salt and light in the world.

PART A

The Christian Entrepreneur

Chapter One

Calling, Purpose, Impact, Authentically Aligned

I am completely honored to be able to co-author this book with eight incredible Christian entrepreneurs who will, in the following chapters, share their entrepreneurial journeys, aha! moments and business advice. But first, I wanted to set the stage of what it means to be a Christian entrepreneur, what makes us different, finding and living your purpose, what ministry is and how it fits in, and what it means to be authentic.

What is a Christian entrepreneur and what makes us different?

There are many definitions of what an entrepreneur is, but put simply …

An entrepreneur is someone that takes some form of risk. Someone who challenges what is, to create something better.

If you are a business owner, chances are you take some form of risk. Entrepreneurship in essence is the creative process of challenging what is and turning it into something fresh, something new. Something that creates new capacity, new solutions and new playing fields.

But what makes us as Christian entrepreneurs different? We see greater purpose, a higher calling in the things we do. A sense of purpose that includes our impact and sphere of influence into what we do day in day out. A love for people that is not easily found in worldly circles, a generous spirit, a peace that passes all understanding, and honorable and empowering business dealings. There is something different about Christians, we carry ourselves differently. When things are in alignment, we stand out, our existence becomes an authentic one.

God, the ultimate creative mastermind, created the earth and everything in it by speaking the different aspects of creation into being and nothing was missed (Genesis 1). We are made in his image.

While some may be more creative than others, each and every person has been given the ability to work, to generate income, to use their skills, to find solutions, to create something new. In a fast paced world such as ours, it's never been more important to be on the cutting edge, in business, ministry and life, and to make sure that we are the best version of ourselves.

Finding and living out your purpose

It's easy to just refer to the different characters of the Bible as just that, characters. Truth is, each person mentioned in the Bible had a purpose, a calling. David was called to be a leader. Solomon was called to build a temple. Deborah was called to be a Judge and to lead an army to victory. And then there's Moses.

Moses

Wow, what a guy. One of the greatest prophets the world has ever seen. God had a plan for his life and even the mass killing of all boys under the age of two in a nation crumbling apart did not stop God's purpose for his life. We read the story to our kids like it was just another 'movie plot', like that basket was a stunt pulled off in the nick of time. But, in reality, we know that God's hand was over every single aspect of that situation.

Found by Pharaoh's daughter, he ended up being raised in royalty. Moses, born in some of the hardest times Israel had faced, was 'set apart' for God, before he even had the ability to save himself or make any decisions. Have you ever been faced with something so big that you couldn't see God ever coming through for you? Remember the basket, the protection and the connection to the higher calling.

The story has many twists and turns, but one day after fleeing for his life from Egypt, God appears to him in a burning bush, telling him that he must return to Egypt to deliver the Israelites from their slavery. Just imagine running from a far than ideal situation, one that questioned his integrity and purpose in life, to be sent back to that very same place to lead God's people out. How would you react?

Not only was he tasked with something most of us will never face in our lifetime, he had to then deliver the Israelites to the promised land. We're talking forty years of doing what God asked without seeing major progress, with a people who went from "God is so good", to "we are all alone" and everything in between many times over, constantly forgetting how God had previously come through for them in every difficulty they had faced.

Mount Sinai was a key development in the story of the Bible and is foundational to our existence today. It was at Mount Sinai, that God gave Moses the law, including the ten commandments. A pivotal moment in history. Moses eventually fulfilled the purpose God had destined him for, but in the meantime, he was doing what God wanted him to do all along. His ministry and impact on the world, was not just seeing the fruition of some big things, God was using him in every season, using him to fulfil that task at hand. He made mistakes, made great gains, had to backtrack and face up to some things, he wasn't perfect, just like we aren't. We can be encouraged that no journey is ever straight forward, in fact, there will be twists and turns, but God can use us in every situation, as we start to unlock our destiny and calling in him. Moses led the Israelites to the edge of their promised land, after much madness! He lived out his calling in God, and today we can remain inspired and encouraged that no matter the path to what God has called us to, he is with us.

We could spend a long time revisiting each character and identifying their God given purpose, but I will leave that research for you to do as you take the time to identify Gods plan your life, or at least the next few steps he would have you take. We may not have the purpose that some of these biblical characters had (some of us are saying "praise God" right now!), but if you are breathing today, God has a plan for your life.

I truly believe that every person born on this earth has a purpose. Some will never know what that is, others will get a glimpse, others know who they are in Christ and what their purpose is and are pursuing and living that purpose out. Even if the what, when, why and how isn't all that clear at certain times, they know that God has a purpose and they actively position themselves for God to lead and guide them to that revelation. Some of us get so busy in the doing, that we forget that there could be more. We get used to what is, but we don't know what we don't know (think about that for a minute).

What lights you up?

You know those people who just seem to be in their element at work? Like they were always destined to be a teacher? Or a doctor? A football or tennis player? Or even a fulltime stay at home mum or dad? It's like they've found their fit in life, many times connecting in with what they wanted to be when they grew up? Their profession or career fits them like a glove comfortably fits a hand. What they do for work seems to come easy, like it was always meant to be? How do they do that? They've aligned their career with who they are as a person. Their passions, their natural interests, the things that light them up. Identifying what you are passionate about, is the first step to help identify your positioning in life.

Add into the mix the intrinsic talents, character traits, spiritual gifts, natural and learned skill sets, the being planted in certain locations for different seasons and the opportunities presented to them. A career or business that incorporates all of these things, becomes the path of least resistance. If you are bored, or struggling at work, or running a business that doesn't completely align with these things, you may need to stop and make some changes. The most successful careers are those that connect in with who you are as a person. The most successful businesses are those that have been founded on this alignment, your passion. Use me as an example.

My passions: Creativity, generating ideas, leadership, empowering people, educating people, being a visionary, being resourceful.

My marketing company started out from a desire to help businesses because I could see there was a need to educate and empower people on how to market themselves creatively, without paying thousands to larger non-personal companies. I started out being passionate about creativity and ideas, then began to run webinars to teach people how to use Facebook, to give them some ideas on how they could use it differently and what they could achieve (vision building). I didn't go to university to study marketing, I was at home with twin babies and a three year old at the time!

I would never have chosen marketing as my preferred career, I somehow fell into it by initially aligning with one of my passions. Marketing is such a creative industry that pulls together all my passions and I now make my sole income from that one business. I stand out from other marketing companies as I was not trained to do things a certain way, I just chose to continually learn and embrace what was in front of me. I do things differently by working out what the client needs individually, I break the marketing rules sometimes (ethically!) and I get results in ways that other companies can't. The things that light me up, are the things that have been a huge part of my success.

Showing leadership, educating and empowering people are three of my passions, and I've incorporated all of them into what I do. My work is generally connecting in with all my passions. When something doesn't align with these, I sure know about it! They say 'do what you love and you'll never work a day in your life', and I can honestly say that most of the time, what I do, doesn't feel like work.

What are your passions in life? Do you feel that your career or business align with who you are and what you believe you are here to do? It's one thing to be salt and light, it's another to be completely authentically aligned with who you were destined to be, with being salt and light, a natural outcome from the way we live, work, and have impact. Let's talk authenticity.

The Authentic Life – your ministry to the world

Authenticity, it's a buzz word, I know, but it's the best word that actively describes the existence I believe we are destined to have. You see, we compartmentalise the different areas of our lives, we go to work on a Monday and can't wait until Friday comes around (some of us work right on through the weekend!). We 'do' ministry on our allocated days, we spend time with family and friends. We hang out for our next lot of holidays or for the day when we can actually take holidays. Some things feel like harder work than others, there are things that don't feel right, there are things that do. It's all part of this experience we call 'life'.

But what if there was a better way? A way to create a new norm, a different way to live your best life, to fulfil that role that God has for you, day in day out, as you manage your business or work? What if your ministry, career, service, influence and impact could all be aligned and you felt at ease because everything was working authentically? The good news is, it can. It will involve a mindset change, a decision to develop new strategies, a commitment to a new path, reshuffling of some things, and the determination to create a new norm in your life that will see you not only living your best life, but also really bringing out your best and excelling in every area.

In church circles we talk about doing questionnaires to work out what our spiritual gifts are. We work out how we can best serve on a Sunday or through the church week of events, but we don't take it far enough. All of those things are super important and can help identify where you best serve in your church, but what if you considered those gifts in every other part of your life? What if your spiritual gifts were outworked in your business or workplace, too? What we are talking about is considering all these God given gifts in the realm and outworking of your business and workplace. An aligned existence.

It comes back to that authentic life, one that is in flow, where you are everything you were created to be. Where Sunday through to Saturday night, is one authentic existence, without chopping and changing from the secular workplace to the Christian doing ministry. The strength of who you are as a person, spiritually, mentally and emotionally, becomes the foundation of your impact on the world around you, all while paying the bills and working towards the life of your dreams.

You know what it's like when a certain bone is out of place or a muscle is inflamed or when you can't use a hand or a foot because of injury? It really brings to the forefront the fact that something is not what it should be or where it should be. It causes discomfort and you have to change the way you do things to accommodate that. Some of us can put up with injury or discomfort better than others, but it should never be long term. The same goes with our authentic existence.

It's natural for things to feel out of whack at different times but life can't go on indefinitely like that. It might be that something doesn't quite fit anymore or that it's not working with the other factors in play. You may have grown out of your current business or career and chosen to embrace something else. It presents a great opportunity for you to pay attention to what's not working and make that change. We need to aim for alignment in our lives.

We take certain hats off and put others on and it takes it toll. Why? Because we get busy doing so much, flicking between this and that and it gets tiring. Imagine living an authentic life, one where you know what lights you up and what doesn't. Where you know who you are, what your strengths are and what you've been put here to do (in some way or another). Where you get so used to identifying the things that stir your passion, that you know what is and what isn't a good fit for you, that you become able to just flow through your week knowing God can use you at any point.

> Authenticity = alignment with who you are in Christ + your purpose/calling + your God given spiritual giftings + skills + passions.

Not sure what God's plan for your life is? Start taking some form of action and God will continue to reveal to you as you seek him prayerfully.

Authenticity + Business
If authenticity is aligned with you as a person, how does this tie in with running a successful business? Good question! Here's the thing: the very foundation of a business starts with a person, right? Someone has an idea, sees a need, needs work or a new career path and so we find ourselves starting a business. But don't just monetise your passions, consider how you can monetise who you are, your uniqueness. How can you market that unique, authentic you to the world, or incorporate that into what you do?

The success of your business begins with you.

The direction of your business is initially determined by you.

The culture of your business is created by you.

The earning capacity of your business depends on many things, starting with your skill set, expectation and ideals around money.

The income level of your business is most often directly related to your mindset and any blocks you have around money.

The growth of your bottom line is directly determined by your decisions.

The driving force behind your business is initially you.

The evolving of a business and its growth begins with your ability to change and embrace it, or not.

The word of mouth factor begins with how you treat your clients and how you serve them.

What is ministry exactly and how does it align with The Christian Entrepreneur?

Let's face it, we can't all be pastoring churches. We can't all be running charities and be missionaries overseas. If we were all leaders, tied up in running churches, charities or missions projects, how would we connect with the world as much as we do? It's time we reshaped the way we think about ministry, as this ties in 100% with authentic living and, believe it or not, your business or career. I want to propose that we have a massive opportunity to impact and influence those around us, while we are on the ground. It's not about Bible bashing, it's about being real. People connect with that. I love it that I get to run a business, speak at different events, serve clients and have an impact on those around me, without walking into church on a Monday. Ministry is your impact on the world around you. There is nothing more refreshing than coming across someone who is so centered and grounded in something bigger than themselves.

Ephesians 2:10b (TEV) says *"In our union with Christ Jesus he has created us for a life of good deeds, which he has already prepared for us to do"*. These "good deeds" are our service to the world. It's the how, what, why and where of service. Ministry, is simply service. Faithful service to God and to others on his behalf. Bible.org, defines ministry as …

> *'The faithful service of God's people rendered unto God and others on His behalf to bring Him glory, build up His church, and reach out to His world.'*

Ministry is service with a higher purpose.

Ministry is what we do, how we do it, and why.

Ministry can be the way people recognise there is something different about you.

Ministry is helping those around us, connect to God.

It's weird that I remember sitting in church as a kid, being told that church is not a Sunday thing, it's a Sunday to Saturday thing, which kind of made sense. That we are called to be 'the church' every day of the week. It wasn't until I hit my 30's that I had a real revelation of this. Sounds basic I know, but all of a sudden I realised that everything I am, everything I do, everything I give, is my ministry to the world.

In workshops, we teach people that their branding is not just their logo and marketing collateral, it's also the way they present themselves, how their staff treat people, how they deal with complaints, how they deal with the good and the bad. The way we live matters. The way we respond, act and carry ourselves, matters. We are God's hands and feet. Our greatest impact is not the words we speak, it's the way we live.

This line of thinking not only took away my disappointment of not being in 'full time ministry', it also enabled me to feel incredibly empowered to be my best, to give my best and to have a positive influence on the world around me. I was in 'ministry', serving those around me with everything I had. I finally felt energised and passionate because living my best life was actually my message and impact on the world. It was a real, authentic existence that made a difference just by me being who I was. The world needs more authentic people. People who are real, people who live their best life. That is what people will recognise and that is what they will connect with.

In business I teach that 'people connect with people'. This creates huge opportunity for God to use us in the littlest of ways right through to the big situations. The person we become, the influence we can have on one single person, the way we carry ourselves, our successes and failures, God uses it all. There is nothing that stands out more in our world today, than seeing a group of people living truly authentic purposeful lives, with vision, tenacity, joy and peace. We are on the ground, running successful businesses doing the very things we are passionate about and impacting those around us.

Excellence

So if we are living out God's purpose for our lives day in day out, and the way we act and do business contributes to an authentic life in line with God's plans, then we also have an incredible responsibility for excellence. I have a responsibility, that as an important part of the kingdom of God, and the 'church', I need to be and offer my best, to live an authentic life 24/7, not just when I feel like it. My life is a message. That's huge. It's excellence that makes you stand out in a crowd. It's excellence that encourages you to keep growing, to keep learning, to upskill and work on the areas that need work. It's excellence that stands out, and keeps the clients and customers coming back to you over and over again. It's excellence that has people referring you onto their friends.

Just because you are a pastor, worship leader, youth leader, missionary or award winning entrepreneur doesn't mean you stop learning, pushing yourself, pursuing excellence. No-one is ever 'there', we can always be better.

Food for thought

Have you identified your calling? If so, write it down and begin to pray into that calling, asking God for opportunity, revelation, open doors and the right people in your life. If not, talk to a trusted friend, pastor, mentor or coach and identify what God has called you to.

If you feel guilty about wanting to be successful with a large income, identify where those feelings are coming from. What do you need to do to overcome them?

Does your church and ministry team support and encourage you in your business? If not, what can you do about it?

Consider how you can serve people through your business and thereby express your ministry.

How does being a Christian set you apart from your competitors?

What are your beliefs about wealth. Do you think it is acceptable for a Christian to be wealthy? What does scripture say about wealth?

How can you be more authentic and express the essence of who you are through your business.

What do you really need from your church and what do they need from you as salt and light in the world.

PART B

The Christian Entrepreneur

Chapter Two

Giving Wings to Magnificent Dreams

I am an entrepreneur who loves to dream BIG. God gave Joseph a dream but that dream was not fulfilled overnight, nor was it a linear 10 step plan going from A to J. As you develop in your relationship with the Lord you soon learn that God's ways are not always our ways, His ways are higher. What we thought would defeat us, God turns into victory. That which we thought would define us, God uses for breakthrough and our battle scars become testimonies that point others to the Cross.

I do not like to be put in a box or to define myself in under a sentence. I find it hard because I simply love to put my hand to many things and I love to do a number of those things through the vehicle of business. It is the way that I am wired and it took me years to finally be comfortable with who I was, throwing off the restraints of what others said I should or could be. Only my God in His mercy has lead me on this path of healing and loving the many parts that make up me and though it might seem somewhat of a jigsaw puzzle, God knows exactly what the final picture needs to look like.

My passion that flows through every aspect of what I do in my businesses is the desire to pour strength, encouragement and hope into the core of other's dreams – no matter what shape that dream may be as in a career, a business, a hobby, a study opportunity and so on. I believe in every God-given dream there lays the latent power to change the world. God has called us to collaborate with Him as a world changer, a history maker, that His name be lifted high. I have learned that if we but shift our thinking and take a first step in the right direction, any dream is possible. Yes, the outworking of any dream takes guts, determination, struggle, prayer, tears, heartache and pain, but my God is well able. He can do exceedingly above that which I ask or think.

The waiting room is a powerful place!

Yes, your dream is possible! I was once locked in the stingy confines of a small thinking world but with strength, encouragement and hope I am flying: soaring free and learning to fly higher, wider, and deeper little by little. I don't want these wings clipped and I don't want to ever be one who clips the wings of another, because we were created to fly with the gifts, talents, skills and personality that God has given us.

> 'As we wait upon the Lord we shall renew our strength and mount up as wings like eagles, we shall run and not be weary, we shall walk and not faint.'

I have grown to understand the waiting room is a powerful place as God works in His ways to transition us from one step to the next step with the dream He has put in our hearts. God's timing is always perfect – though He does seem to have a habit of making it the last minute before midnight.

Where I would once grow very anxious as to whether something would happen or come through, I have learned instead to turn my mind to anticipating and expecting how things will work out and what God will do.

As a young girl, I had the advantage of a great education. I was always encouraged to read, write, learn, solve mathematical problems and excel in the school environment. I will always be grateful to my parents for giving me this gift of an immense love for learning – because it is this thread that runs through every part of what I do in life. You will always find me reading some article or book, asking curious questions, pondering, thinking, brainstorming and problem solving.

However, one thing that was lacking in my childhood was a perception of emotional love and connection. I felt for many years that I was unloved, unwanted; that I was some type of nuisance and that I needed to stay silent because what I had to say or the ideas I had did not matter or were not going to be of good to anyone. I was very shy, reserved and timid as a girl, always too afraid to try something new or to make new friends. We were never allowed to play with or have friends around, to go on school camps and excursions and we rarely had family members visit us.

Imagine if all our dreams could fly!

Growing up as a young woman was not easy. I always seemed at a disadvantage and marginalised. I constantly felt that I was on the outside looking in and that I was not free. I felt like a bird trapped inside a cage and I longed to get out of the cage and fly.

I wasn't overly confident and I didn't know how to interact well with groups of people. As a teenager, I spiralled into an emotional rollercoaster of anorexia, depression and suicide attempts. BUT God!

I was brought up in a Catholic household so I understood who Jesus was but I didn't understand that He really cared about me or desired to have a personal loving relationship with me. In my late teens, a couple of school friends encouraged me with their faith journey in God and I started to find that personal faith path for myself.

This strengthened me and helped me to make healthier choices with my life and I began to take hold of the dream I felt burning on the inside of me.

My experiences as a girl and young woman shaped me into a person with a strong desire to be a spokeswoman for others in situations of injustice, to be a voice for girls and women who do not have a voice. My love for education led me to a teaching career and then into the fields of law and entrepreneurship.

Teaching has empowered me to find my voice, the law has empowered me to speak into situations of injustice and being a business woman has enabled me to put on those wings and finally fly free: out of the cage and into the fullness and joy of what life must offer.

What I can say from my experiences, is that we all have a journey that we are on, we all have a story that is being weaved and shaped as we do life. I thank God that He chooses to walk alongside us if we reach out to Him. Our life journey can be filled with difficulties but it is the lessons within the journey that bring together the pieces of the dream that lies dormant on the inside of each one of us.

Many people choose to allow that dream to remain hidden or undiscovered. I want my journey to inspire you: that as you live out your God-given dreams, you will find it opens doors and opportunities that many of you thought were locked.

Imagine if all the potential within every person young and old were released? Can you picture how that would change our world?

My dream is to empower a generation of business owners to create and design sustainable, heart-centred, values-based businesses. *YOUR BUSINESS DREAM CAN FLY.*

It is time to act on the dreams God has placed in your heart!

I stand with you today to champion you in your dream. My whole purpose is this: to tap on your cage – to bind a broken wing, to breathe in fresh courage, to nudge you into flight.

I ask from you just ONE thing: an empty cage. I want to see you flying and then for you to go and do the same for others – to tap on their cage so that like you, their dream can fly too.

Let's get flying!

To be in business you need to think long term – momentum in business does not happen overnight. The saying 'a fine wine takes time' can be just as aptly applied in business – a fine business takes time. Here are my:

5 top building blocks for activating sustainable momentum in your business.

Building Block 1: PLAN and PRIORITISE

- If you fail to plan, you are planning to fail *(Benjamin Franklin)*
- Create a 90-day plan. Divide your calendar year into three months/per quarter or per term or into nine to twelve week chunks. 90 days is twelve weeks.
- Set targets for sales, marketing, clients, strategy/vision, financial growth. Keep this to no more than four to six targets which are very specific.
- In order to achieve your targets what do you need to do? For example, to achieve your $ sales amount, then how many clients, customers or packages, etc. do you need to sell?
- What marketing do you need to implement to achieve your targets? e.g. attending X number of networking events, promoting a facebook advertising campaign, doing a postcard mail box drop, developing a landing page for one of your products or services.
- In each 90-day period create a new product or add on a new service or vary a package you may have – to be ready to launch in the subsequent 90-day period.

- Determine the amount of time those targets will take? For example, measuring your marketing statistics may mean you need to diarise in a two-hour block of time once a fortnight to do this.

- When planning, think in terms of blocks of time and break your targets into billable and non-billable hours.

- Prioritise the billable hours – you cannot do everything in a three-month period and you do have to make money in your business, so billable hours/sales are important. You can't just spend your whole-time planning!

- Are your non-billable hours too high? Can you outsource? Is there enough billable hours for outsourcing the non-billable e.g. hiring a virtual assistant at $30 an hour versus you coaching a client for an hour at $110?

- Measure, measure and measure again much like you would do if you wanted to create an award-winning meal. Each week keep track of your marketing statistics e.g. number of fans, engagement from website, number on email list, people attending your meetup group.

- Always remember: it is about working smarter and not harder. Commit to an end of quarter review and then a beginning of quarter plan at around three hours for each.

- Break your three-month plan into weeks – what do you need to do each week to meet your target, so if the target is one new client a week, what will that involve?

- Aim for at least thirty minutes to one hour of client-generating activity for four days a week: email, referral, phone call, offer.

Building Block 2: CREATE PROCESSES

- With everything you do in business, work towards creating a process for it. This will mean that what you do is systemised and automated and not reactive and ad-hoc. This can take time to do – but the result is well worth it.

- Example – what is your process after you have attended a network event? Remember networking is not about chasing or spamming. Focus instead on generosity and what you can do to assist the person you are building a relationship with.

- Thus, for instance, your process may be to enter card details into your client database *(yes, you do need to have one of these)*, write a connection email *(send a freebie/complimentary helpful downloadable or one or two links that may be useful to their business)*, identify a referral you can initiate *(introduce via a facebook message or email)*, and then decide on the follow-up action you will do *(e.g. coffee)*. Diarise this as a reminder.

- The key with processes is to use a range of apps and digital tools to help you achieve your goals – I have lots of favourites! My top 3 are **Pocket** for collecting articles and information, www.getpocket.com; **Trello** where I keep my ideas, planning and client notes, www.trello.com; and **Dropvox** which is audio on the run. When I am in a hurry, I can speak my notes, blog ideas etc and the audio is sitting in my Dropbox later for when I am ready to use it. Dropvox is linked to your Dropbox account.

- Processes can drive some business owners spare – get help if you need it and remember it is about efficiency and sustainability. You can't be all things to all people, so you must find better ways to do things.

- Use Scheduling tools for your social media because that sure can take up a lot of time e.g. for twitter I use **Twuffer** and for Instagram I use **latergram**, from my phone.

Building Block 3: PRODUCTISE

- There are only so many hours in a day and our business should not consume us. For service based businesses, think about how you can productise your services, so the service becomes a product – which gets you out of the picture and turns your service into a form of passive income.

- Types of income streams: active (1 to 1), leverage (one to many), hybrid of active and leverage (e.g. Online course but with mastermind or facebook group), passive (e.g. downloadable templates and check sheets) and recurring (e.g. monthly fees from a membership site or retainer fee for monthly client).

- As a new business, you will find a lot of your income will initially come from active services – you simply must get runs on the board and get your brand known for people to see, know and understand what it is you do and what you can offer. As your business grows you can then move to leverage (1 to many vs 1 to 1) and then the wider goal is to move towards productising so that you have passive and recurring income.

- Start small (the walls of Jericho did not come down overnight!) – for instance, templates and checklists that could then move to an online course.

- Remember to teach what you know. Pass on your knowledge, wisdom, and insight. God has gifted it to you, not so you can hide it away but so you can give out of the storehouse He has put inside of you.

- There will only ever be one you. What is your message that you want to spread to the world. What is it of God's heart has He given you to declare in particular, for example – justice.

Building Block 4: CREATE PROJECTS and PROJECT MANAGE

- Plan your business development and growth in terms of projects. Doing so is a good way to keep your ideas flowing but captured, as you can't be working on all your projects at once.

- As an entrepreneur, you always have ideas flowing which can be both an advantage and a disadvantage. I have found putting those ideas into a project format means even if I don't get around to it straight away, I have a means of retaining those thoughts and plans.

- Ideally, have no more than two or three projects per quarter, this will of course depend on the extent of the projects. For example, for one quarter, your three projects could be: developing a product, collaboration with person X and a video workshop series.

- Divide your projects across your income streams (e.g. one active income generation, one leveraged income generation and one passive income generation).

- The next step is then to manage the projects – what is required for each project, what tools are needed, who do I need to seek help from, what can I outsource, how much time will I dedicate to it, what will be the return on investment (ROI – if I need to spend $500 on this project what is it that I am expecting back, e.g. 10 new clients, $2000 sales and so on), how long will I need to wait or am I prepared to wait for the ROI?

- Most importantly ACTION the project plan. REMEMBER action builds momentum, momentum fuels further action.

- Use project management tools e.g. Asana, Wunderlist or Trello or a piece of butcher paper and sticky notes. Find a way that works for you.

- Projects can expand. You can often begin on one project and then other ideas and thoughts pop up, so a way to overcome this challenge is break the project down into phases – when phase one is executed then you can move on to phase two. You need to be disciplined. Accountability is a key, e.g. hire a business coach or join a mastermind group otherwise you will find your projects (i.e. your business development and growth) will always remain incomplete.

Building Block 5: PRACTISE, PRACTISE, AND PRACTISE SOME MORE!

- Just go do it: get out and practise, practise, practise. Take that first step and watch as you do the possible, your God will do the impossible. I have seen this happen repeatedly.

- Over analysis and anxiety leads to paralysis and procrastination. (The deer in the headlights!)

- Open the door just a little, even if the key seems stiff in your hand and then watch God fling open the door to wide open pastures before you. You have to START. You will stumble, trip, fall over and then rise again but remember – 'He that is in you is greater than He that is in the world'.

- For example – networking. How will people get to know about your product and services unless they get to know you, because it's 'you, your story' they are buying. To do sustainable business you need to be a lover of people. If you are an introvert then create a strategy. You could use prompt cards for conversation starters, start with smaller groups or go with a buddy. Get out from behind your computer and press the flesh.

- Ask God to expand your heart for people. *'God looked upon the multitudes and His heart was moved with compassion'*. It is my prayer that as I look upon the people that God puts in my life my heart will be moved towards them.

- Another example is creating video for your business. Video content marketing is the buzz and will continue to be so for some time. If you hate doing video then start with a ten second video on how you love your cat or dog or children and send it to a friend and then build your video confidence muscles from there just like you build your faith muscles, little by little.

- Simply take that one step, for example, buy a desk tripod to put your phone on for filming or buy a nice scarf or new lipstick for filming.

- As a Christian entrepreneur, we are taking ground for the kingdom. We are expanding the kingdom of heaven here on earth as we step out daily into the business realms that God has positioned us in.

Our God is victorious and the battle belongs to Him!

Being a business owner and a Christian is NOT two separate things. My faith is the very core and centre of who I am as a business owner: my values, the way I operate, how I might work with clients and customers. I am a missionary in the business sector. I am a minister of the gospel taking His name into places where others may not have the opportunity to do so.

It does not mean that I don't swear or get upset over clients who don't pay, or that every plan and idea I activate works. No, what it does mean is that the Holy Spirit is there as my helper directing and guiding me, when chaos, turmoil and disappointment may come (and yes it does!). He is my peace. He is the storm chaser who will summon the armies of heaven to do battle on my behalf.

Below is a prophetic word that I wrote in May of this year (2017). I wrote it ten days after I had a major operation, having been diagnosed with stage one uterine cancer. This took me to a very deep dark place of despair. I felt God had always promised my hubby and me children. I have been pregnant twice but miscarried both times. Now here I was at 50, still holding on to that promise. I felt God had said we would be like Sarah and Abraham – that even in our old age, He would make a way.

The irony of it is that I am a passionate and trained Child Protection Practitioner and Lawyer and previously a high school teacher, and my husband is a beautiful Fijian Chief with a love and capacity to nurture children and young people. Now, I felt like all my dreams were smashed – and why had I bothered to use what God had given me. Maybe this whole being an entrepreneur was just some pipe dream that was a fantasy in my mind and not something knitted in the depths of my heart.

And then I remembered Joseph, to whom God gave a dream of the sun, the moon and the stars bowing down to him, yet from that time of the dream until it was fulfilled, Joseph went through the experiences of the pit, Potiphar's house and prison. And there in prison, it seemed even the butler and the candle maker forgot him, BUT our God does not forget. Our God does not fail in the dream that He has put in our hearts. As Joseph's brothers came before him, he spoke to them, *"The enemy meant this for evil, but my God has turned it to good"*.

God's Word and Vision to Me:
'For the weight of His MORNING GLORY will fall and it will cover the earth, not one of the promises of God will be broken. All around us we will hear the trumpet blowing, beginning first in Israel and that trumpet sound will bring the WALLS DOWN that people have put around their lives, those walls will fall and shatter.

This is the picture I saw: people one moment going about their day and then they just stopped and the scene changed. Each person's masks, pains, burdens and intense deep disappointments were revealed and these pains, burdens etc. fell like walls off them until all that was left was a bloodied, bruised, and battered person with no strength to stand or with air in their lungs.

Before me was now this carnage of people: the most horrific battle scene. Blood everywhere, parts of limbs, broken weapons and so on. There was blackness and an eerie silence, all life had been sucked from the air, smoke swirled about, it was cold, so miserable and bleak; hopelessness settled itself as a blanket over this carnage scene.'

'I said, "Lord, what of this battle field?" He replied, "Simply be still, and watch now what I will do. The enemy has come thus far but he shall come no further. Man will look at this carnage field and toss it aside for worthless rubble and rubbish but no one knows the day and the time in which my MORNING GLORY WILL FALL and HOPE will arise. Hope that will seep back into the pores of the people, hope that a new day comes indeed and surely will and has dawned."

"And in that moment, and in that time, and in that place and places my MORNING GLORY will bring to life again that which the night has stolen. I will restore, I will make whole, I will mend; as in a moment of time the stench and intensity of the battle will no longer be remembered for death has NO sting, the victory is and will always be mine."'

God never gives up on us, always remember that! Life happens to us all, the good and the darn hard! As Christians, we are not immune from pain and suffering and disappointments BUT in Him there is hope: hope that is the anchor of our souls.

As I started this chapter I spoke of how our dreams do not take a nice linear ten step path and in sharing some of my story you will see that certainly is so. Yes, I love to plan, but I have come to understand that He is the Master Planner and the Master Builder. As I step out each day with the measure of faith in my hand (even if it is just the size of that mustard seed) my God will show up in His mercy and faithfulness.

To the victory of your dreams: my God, your God is well able! Love Maree xx

MAREE CUTLER-NAROBA

Contributor Profile: Maree is a multi-skilled Business Strategist and Educator, Digital Content Writer and Child Protection Practitioner/Lawyer, who is also affectionately known as The Ideas Guru. She uses a range of styles and methods to provide information, insights and ideas to management, staff, students and clients that is relevant, practical, creative and timely.

Self Introduction: God-lover on a mission to help as many women as I can give wings to their business and career dreams AND a passionate advocate for the protection of children from abuse and neglect.

Websites: www.mareecutlernaroba.com and www.boomersbizgym.com

Facebook: ideas2propelu

Linkedin: Maree Cutler Naroba

Instagram: maree_cutler_naroba

Email: mcnaroba@gmail.com

Digital Content Writer: www.businesscontentwriter.online

Child Protection Practitioner: www.childprotectiondownunder.com.au

Founder – The Deborah Conference: www.facebook.com/thedeborahconference

Founder – Women Echo Him Ministries: www.facebook.com/groups/1395829894008932

Food for thought

What past experiences do you feel might be holding you back? What will you do about those experiences? Who can you talk to?

What past experiences have developed inner strength and character?

List your strengths, abilities, talents and passions. How can you use them in your business?

What is the dream God has placed in your heart? Have you written it down?

Maree lists five building blocks for activating sustainable momentum in your business. Depending on the stage you are at in your business, decide on which building block to work on next. You might need to start at the beginning or you may already be at building block three. Write this building block down. Spend some time praying about this and ask God for His leading and guidance. Now, break this building block down into small, easily implemented steps. Find someone to help you do this if necessary. This process will put you on the road to progress; all you need to do now is implement each small step. Then you will be ready to move on to the next building block.

Chapter Three
Finding Freedom

As I sat there in the middle of the church auditorium, tears streaming down my cheeks, my concerned husband looking on and listening to the woman who had posed a question that got me "ugly crying" in the first place, I felt angry.

Angry at everyone around me, angry at this woman sitting in front me, angry at my husband for not protecting me, angry at God for all the unanswered prayers and angrier at the thought that I might have to go around this mountain yet another time.

"Enough! Enough! I have had enough, God. Enough!", I cried. "I've been around this mountain so many times, I'm simply not prepared to go around it again".

"What exactly do you want from me, God?", I silently asked, followed by, "What exactly is it that I am supposed to do?"

The answers to these questions did not show up immediately. Not that I expected them to. In the weeks to follow I came to an understanding that I wasn't going around the mountain again but rather, in my circling I was higher toward the top. The mountain peak was getting closer each time I circled.

One step closer to a business and life I desired or so I thought. God wasn't done with me yet. If there is anything that I can attest to it is that entrepreneurship puts hair on your chest, metaphorically speaking, of course. In my opinion entrepreneurship is one of the best personal development programs a person can do.

No doubt this has been my experience. I have been stretched beyond my comfort zone at times. More times than I would like to admit, even to the point of quitting. But here I am, sharing my messy story with you. No quitting for me and I hope this story inspires you to keep on going, too. Onward, upward, not just round and round in circles but circling on to the top of your mountain.

Please do read between the lines as there are many parts I am not able to include but with a little insight you may glean more from my story than what is written. My prayer is that my story will inspire confidence and ignite courage in your walk.

Patience cultivates resilience!
Patience has never been one of my strong suits. When I started my business I expected to realise immediate results and instant success. Little did I know that I would need to dig so deep, be as patient and cultivate extreme resilience before my dream became a reality.

In time it became apparent, with few sales, a small list of clients I could count on one hand and an ever growing list of courses saved to my computer hard drive, that my business was not going to grow into the million-dollar overnight success I had hoped. In fact, it would take years to even earn an income relative to one I earned in a nine-to-five job. It seemed that I had become a professional course goer, signing up for one course after another and often not completing these courses or worse, not implementing all I had learned.

In time I realised that I was not alone in this. Purchasing course after course, not taking action, experiencing frustration and feeling overwhelmed seemed to be endemic to the online world. If I was struggling with this, how many others were experiencing the same thing but were too afraid to voice their frustrations out loud?

How many others were sitting on the other side of my computer screen wearing a bulletproof mask and presenting a happy face to the world when in reality they were filled with uncertainty and frustration, unsure of where to turn to next?

Feelings of dismay washed over me. I felt so alone.

I had just about had it. I was so tired of going around in circles, jumping from one marketing strategy to the next in the hope that one of these would stick, all the while pretending to be this successful entrepreneur that clearly I was not. Yet, I had a compelling desire to be the owner of an internationally recognised business serving and speaking to people all over the world.

This was my incredible dream:

To inspire people to connect to their dreams and ideas that expand who they can be in the world and then to encourage them to confidently take inspired and courageous action to fulfil those dreams

I wasn't about to give this up.

Connector of Dreams

Months later, I recalled a dream I had a few years prior to the ugly crying incident. I remembered the words I thought I had heard God say, "Build a faith based business."

I wondered what a 'faith based business' looked like. I had an uneasy feeling I was not going to like what I was about to uncover. A 'faith based business' sounded like a lot of hard work and a lot of faith. Now, I wasn't afraid of hard work and I had heaps of faith but still I questioned whether it would be enough.

I wasn't even sure whether I had heard this or whether this 'faith based business' dream was just that, a silly dream. Was it just too much pizza the evening before or an idea impressed on my unconscious mind because of a discussion with someone?

I sensed it was none of the above. Faith is what is required to grow a faith based business or any business for that matter. As much as I wanted it to be different, this was it! No more controlling, hustling or trying to push things into place. No more doubting, wondering or wishing things would be better.

I needed an entirely different perspective. I was ready to try anything. Everything else I had tried previously had achieved minimal results. I had nothing to lose. I was ready to give it my best and last shot.

I'm not sure whether you have been in a situation where it feels a little like you're in between a rock and a hard place, with little room to manoeuvre. Low on funds and even lower on confidence, self-doubt reared its ugly head and I seriously focused on dropping the entire business idea.

I didn't even know if I was cut out to be an entrepreneur. The harsh reality was that I was also 'technically unemployable'. With very little hands-on work experience in Australia, I found my applications rejected one after the other.

Ten, twenty, thirty job applications, if not more, all in a period of a few months. My sense of identity, self-worth and belief in my capabilities were nose diving and heading for the sharp rocks in the distance far below.

Even if I had really wanted to find a job (which deep down, I really didn't) I was unable to get one. Each interview led to the same outcome. "You're too qualified for this position. You will be bored within a few months."

Gifts come in all forms – mine came in the form of a 'NO'.

The Missing Piece

Who would I need to be to grow this business? Who would I need to be to attract my most aligned clients? Clients who would pay me, not only what I thought I was worth, but for the transformation I could bring to their life or business?

I knew deep down that I was not that person, YET! – In becoming clearer on my dream business, my services and who I was meant to serve, I also identified a huge gap: The missing piece of the puzzle.

That missing piece, the gap I identified, was **ME.**

I needed to change, to become the person I was created to be!

I had been so busy following other people's processes that I had lost sight of who I needed to be to attract my ideal client.

I was filled with fear and I had allowed this fear to stop me from honestly expressing my true self in the world. Fear of rejection, failure, success, judgment, not being able to deliver, not fitting in, not belonging, being the same as everyone else, not being unique enough, my own thoughts and being found out to be a fake.

Now, don't get me wrong, I wasn't walking around a nervous wreck. As a matter of fact no one would be any wiser. I was outwardly confident going about my daily tasks. I just donned my safety mask and my bullet proof vest and never let on that inside of me was this struggle. It was a struggle to release the authentic, talented me that was hidden beneath the surface, the real me. I was in the midst of an identity crisis.

I started to lose focus and I withdrew more and more, making up excuses and pretending that I was in a period of 'rest', 'creation' and 'reinvention'. I avoided going out, networking or meeting with friends or colleagues who knew me well. I just wasn't up to the scrutiny, the questions or the perceived judgment and shame I felt at 'not making it'.

> *I needed time to find myself,*
> *to re-align, re-define and re-invent.*

It was GAME ON. Now it was time for me to discover who I was and what I was meant to create. To uncover my skills, to develop my gifts and let go of all those excuses and past mistakes that I continued to bring out just to remind myself how far I was from actually achieving all that I had set out to achieve.

> **I knew I was playing small.
> I understood the immense potential that lay within!**

No matter how hard I tried I couldn't seem to move from this stuck place I found myself in, swinging between self-doubt and massive confidence.

Not long after receiving my 'build a faith based business' dream I received a word.

ESTHER

Now, for those of you who have heard of the story of Esther (born Hadassah) in the Bible you will know that she was taken from a place of obscurity as an orphan in her uncle Mordecai's home and placed in a position of prominence in the king's palace where her position provided her with the opportunity to save a nation.

So what does this story have to do with building a business?

The story of Esther has been a wonderful inspiration to me in my life and my business. When you read the full story of Esther you will come to realise that there is so much more to the story than meets the eye.

A young girl moved from a place of obscurity into a position of prominence. Her story is one of bravery, courage, faith, obedience, being in the right place at the right time and stepping into her true identity as a queen.

Even while writing this, I sense a shift in my emotions and I am yet again reminded of the incredible insights from her story that apply directly to growing my business. Golden nuggets, that as my gift, you can apply to your life and business too.

1. WHAT YOU SEEK IS INSIDE YOU.

Right now you may be feeling a little like Esther: secret, hidden, even obscure. No one really knows you, your talents, your gifts, what you are capable of or how you can be of service to others. Too often we downplay our own skills, strengths and talents. You may have done this too. You may have wondered "what do I have to offer someone else that they will pay for?"

Plenty, beautiful entrepreneur.

You have plenty to give and plenty to offer. What you are seeking is right under your nose. Your gifts are closer than you think. Too often we discount the talents that come naturally to us because they are so close to home. We do these things so well that we no longer consider that others may struggle with what we find so easy to do.

But there it is: your gift, the one you have not noticed. The one thing that when people ask you to help them with it, you almost say "That old thing – anyone can do that".

Take a moment to consider: What is it that you do so well? What is it that you are really passionate about that given an opportunity you could speak about it for a week? What words do your friends, family and colleagues use when they describe you? List them all. While you may find more than one word has been used, a common thread will usually emerge pointing to the one stand out quality or ability that perfectly characterizes you.

Yes, there are many people who may be able to do the thing that you do but only YOU can do it the way you do it. That makes you unique with your flair, your style.

In saying this, if others could do what you do so well why on earth do they ask you to help them? Simply because you have what it is that they want and only you can deliver it in the way that is uniquely you.

This is your one thing, Child of God. In my work with my incredibly talented clients we address this in more detail, looking into their story, stance, stand, style and strengths. Most days a few light bulbs go off when they realise just how close they are to the one thing that makes them stand out in the market place. Don't discount the things that you do so naturally as something not worthy of being monetised.

It may take a little digging or someone to help you shine a light on those incredible qualities and gifts you have that have been hidden for so long but when they're uncovered they have the ability to change lives.

2.   PREPARATION BEFORE PROGRESS.
Esther had to prepare to become the woman she was created to be. As Hadassah, she wasn't in the right place nor did she have the correct frame of mind to do what was required of her. She had to go through a process of preparation, beautification and discovery to uncover her true identity.

Knowing who she was enabled her to make decisions that only a queen could make, despite the fact that there was considerable risk involved and the actions she took could have resulted in her losing her life.

I realise that this may be a little extreme in today's terms but here's the thing: To be successful in business, there will always be a process of preparation and discovery of your true identity and a time to develop the vision. But there will come a time when you will need to make some tough decisions and take some nail-biting action in order to achieve your goals.

Strategy alone is not enough!

Each day online entrepreneurs, coaches, consultants, authors and speakers are using social media to increase their visibility and to connect more with people who may be their ideal client.

From my own experience having worked online for the past six plus years I have found that strategies that used to work well, after a while no longer worked. The speed at which things are changing online is moving faster and faster. More people are starting businesses and joining the online noise daily.

The result of this is a busy news feed if you're using Facebook, never ending chatter from Twitter as well as keeping up with posts on LinkedIn and Pinterest. Add to this the constant pressure to learn more, know more and remain up to date with the latest marketing strategy. I noticed that incredible women would start businesses and within a few months the fire inside would start to fade and they would slip off the scene.

This got me wondering. I had been there, almost done that and knew that even though strategy was great and necessary it would take more than strategy to keep a person in the game.

To succeed in business, I started to consider that what people really required along with a certain amount of strategy was to uncover their true identity and to build their business from the inside out.

Building a business from the inside out means having a sound inner resolve, a definite why, clarity of vision, confidence, courage and an unstoppable mindset that ties in with a strong sense of identity.

3. UNCOVER YOUR AUTHENTIC IDENTITY

We all have a certain image of ourselves – beliefs about the kind of person we are. Having a strong sense of identity, a clear awareness of 'who you are', makes it easier to connect with other likeminded people and groups or as the online world would have it: Your tribe.

People with a strong sense of identity often stand out more and are more memorable but many people seem to spend a lot of time trying to figure out who they are, what they want and what they believe.

Knowing who you are provides clarity and with clarity comes confidence.

Now, I'm not asking you to put yourself in a risky position where you could lose your life like Esther but without first uncovering your true identity, knowing who and whose you are at your core, your business will be a struggle.

You could have been or may even be right now, at this place in your life where you are questioning your own self-worth, your direction, your business model or who you are here to serve. Perhaps you have come full circle and are ready to give up because this dream business you so dearly want to succeed with seems too far from your reach.

It might be time to get back to basics, to uncover your true identity and then to take inspired action from that place.

Queen Esther did it, I did it and you can too.

Everyone seems to have an opinion of who they think you should be!
From the time you are born there is a never ending stream of people trying to tell you who you are meant to be. Parents, teachers, friends, colleagues, grandparents, media and society – it never ends. Everyone seems to have an opinion of who they think you should be and what you should be doing. In the midst of it all is you – just wanting to be you.

Over time, with all the pressure from the external world, our identity seems to get lost, hidden in the 'superstar, exceptional student, high achiever' persona we adopt along the way. Years later we suddenly realise that we have lost the one thing that makes us incredibly valuable: OUR IDENTITY.

Before you can be and do all that you were created for, this issue of identity must be settled in your heart and mind.

Here's one thing I do know: YOU are a child of God. To know this is freedom. To know this is to understand your purpose and to fulfil it.

4.   IT'S ALL IN THE TIMING
Too often we become impatient and try to make things happen quickly. We create programs and offer services simply because everyone else is getting their stuff out there and we may feel compelled to do the same.

'Courage to Bloom' is a program I had been considering for some time. I had it all planned out in my head. I knew exactly what I wanted my clients to experience and how I wanted them to feel.

While it was a brilliant program, the timing was terribly off and sadly the impact that I wanted to make was diminished by a rushed ending as we headed toward the Christmas holidays. All the time, effort and energy I put into getting everything just right was blown right out of the water.

I was left feeling like a fraud and a failure, not to mention that the program ended up being more about strategy (exactly the thing I was trying to avoid) and less about establishing a success mindset while allowing courage to bloom in a way that allowed strategy and heart to meet.

I've learned my lesson and the concept of being in the right place at the right time. Esther knew this. She trusted the process and the perfect moment presented itself for her to do what she was called to do.

Your dream is perfectly timed. Not a moment too soon or a moment too late. When we are fully surrendered to trusting the process, without striving, being impatient or trying to push out a service or program because "everyone else is doing it" we enable ourselves to prepare and know when the timing is right.

My advice to you is to trust that the season you are in, even though it may feel slow or sluggish and you wish it would realise the results you desire sooner, is the perfect season for you.

Success is not the end destination we have all come to believe. Rather, it's the journey we experience, the character that is formed and the joy we have along the way.

God's timing in all things is always on time. When we learn to entrust our businesses, our products and our clients to Him, the end result is one that feels good and aligns with who you are and with your values.

God provides abundantly and with His guidance you can achieve over and above anything you can do on your own.

As you can see, the story of Esther has so many lessons applicable to life and business. In the chapter above we've touched on:

- **What you seek is within you.** You have incredible potential inside of you just waiting to be released. We all have gift and talents. Are you hiding yours?

- **Preparation before progress.** *"Spectacular achievement is always preceded by unspectacular preparation."* – Robert H. Schuller. Your preparation may look kind of messy as did Esther's in the beginning. The outcome though looked entirely different and yours will too. Prepare to be spectacular.

- **Uncover your authentic identity.** How often do we skip this step in our personal development? To get to the core of the onion all outer layers must first be peeled away. This can feel painful and be downright scary. Trust me when I say that the sweetest part is always at the centre.

- **It's all in the timing.** Are you tired of walking around the mountain? Consider this: Joshua circled the wall of Jericho six times with no visible evidence that his efforts to bring down the wall were even working. Be prepared and keep on walking. Esther had no idea of the impact she was going to have on her nation. Your success has its own special time.

I could go on and on sharing more insights that I have drawn from this incredible story. Insights which include surrender, trust, obedience, discipline, confidence and having the courage to bloom but I will leave you with one last golden nugget.

I hope it encourages and inspires you as you follow your dream, as you surrender your life and business to the will of God, as you truly step into who you were created to be and as you have the courage to follow the destiny that only you can complete.

"NEVER GIVE UP ON GOD GIVEN DREAMS"

BRENDA TSIAOUSIS

Contributor Profile: Brenda inspires confidence and ignites courage while helping entrepreneurs globally realise their full potential in life, business and entrepreneurship. She provides a powerful blend of business and life coaching with a core message of the importance of developing "The Courage To Bloom" to a growing community of women in Australia and around the world. She is a Business Potentialist, Author and Speaker, and a highly regarded leader in her field.

Self Introduction: Prolific speaker, green tea lover and proud mum to four beautiful children and wife to her gorgeous Greek husband!

Website: www.brendatsiaousis.com

Facebook: BrendaTsiaousis

Linkedin: Brenda Tsiaousis

Email: BrendaTs@BrendaTsiaousis.com

Food for thought

Are you angry with God, yourself or others?

What do you need to do to find inner peace?

List your fears and discuss them with a trusted friend, mentor or coach. Bring them to God in prayer.

What character traits do you need to have to see your vision realised?

What character traits do you need to work on first?

What masks do you wear in your life and/or business? How can you identify them? How can you remove them?

Do you need counselling from a professional to overcome any issues in your personal life or from the past?

Do you need assistance in dealing with a difficult person or relationship? Can you talk to this person about finding common ground and putting differences aside? If you need help with this, find someone to discuss your options with or perhaps employ the services of a mediator.

How can you deal with 'self-doubt' in a positive way?

Brenda said that she had to re-align, re-define and re-invent. What do these actions mean to you? How will you work these actions out in your life?

Read the book of Esther. Write down any truths or revelations the Holy Spirit shows you?

Chapter Four
What Are You Worth?

The vast majority of photography businesses fail in their first two years. What is the biggest cause of failure? A lot of photographers love being creative and taking images but they neglect the really important things – marketing and pricing.

I was nearly one of those statistics.

I graduated from university with a Bachelor of Science degree at the end of 1997 but I found it difficult to find full-time work. After moving to Brisbane, my parents and I needed employment and we spotted a real estate photography business for sale. I'd done a tiny bit of photography in high school and my dad used to be a real estate agent, so we thought it was a perfect match. I mean, how hard could it be?

However, after paying a lot of money to buy the business as a going concern, we didn't manage things very well. My photography was woeful and the clients were quickly disappearing. After four years of struggling, we almost gave up and packed it in. I even spoke to a real estate agent client about going to work for him.

Nevertheless, we decided that we would give it one more go. I signed up for a full-time photography course, hoping that this would help me with my photography skills. It was our only hope.

After doing a lot of studying and not a lot of paid photography, I graduated from photography school. Now I knew what I was doing, I quickly developed (no pun intended!) some fresh ways of shooting the inside and outside of homes and other buildings, and that's when things really started to take off.

New clients started coming in and pretty soon we were growing so fast we needed to put on a part-time staff member just to handle the photo editing. After another six months we needed to hire someone full-time. Less than a year later we hired another full-time photographer to join our team and then shortly after we needed another photographer, then another. It was a massive turnaround!

However, the photography services could only take our business so far. When a number of new competitors joined our industry I had to learn new skills just to keep our business ahead of the game.

Seek out the wisdom of others.
To help us with our business skills I engaged the services of a business coach to guide us through some turbulent times. That was helpful for a couple of years but then we needed to move on to marketing, so we paid a marketing team to help us for another twelve months.

Getting outside help can be expensive but it's interesting what can happen when we don't rely on ourselves for everything. The unfortunate thing is that a lot of us, and I include myself in this, wait until we can't hang on any longer to admit we need help.

Why do we do that?

We do it in business, we do it when our marriages are shaky and about to collapse and we do it in our spiritual lives when we wait until we completely fall apart before we reach out to God for help.

As someone once said, "Tomorrow – a mystical land where 98% of all human productivity, motivation and achievement is stored."

From what I've seen, one reason why we keep putting off those positive actions is because we don't want to face the negative causes of the pain we feel. So we put it off for later and that feels good to us. We've avoided the pain and we have a plan to deal with it another day. Plan devised and plan completed. We've rewarded ourselves and we feel much better, albeit with negative reinforcement.

We aren't really any better off, because the underlying cause of the problem is still there. When we make it to tomorrow we once again put off that positive action for another day or another month or for an indefinite period of time.

Guidance from others can help us get back on track and keep us accountable!

"I'll reach out to that person next week. Maybe things will improve by then!" It's a story we keep telling ourselves but it's not good for business and it's not good for our spiritual health either.

In reality, seeking out the wisdom of others, especially those who have been down the same path we're treading, is one of the best things we can do. The guidance they can offer and the mistakes they learned from, that they can share with us, can help to get us back on the right track and keep us accountable to do the things that we ought to be doing.

That was one of the biggest lessons I learned during my years as a photographer and is something I wish I'd taken on board much, much sooner.

Know your numbers

"You can't substitute great photography for bad numbers."

That's one of the big statements I try to get across to photographers I'm working with. A lot of them think that either what they do shouldn't cost all that much and they feel embarrassed about charging hundreds of dollars for a set of images or they don't understand the full cost of doing business and undercharge for their services.

I'd have to say that this is one of the biggest mistakes I see from a lot of business people, with too many businesses not charging enough for their products or services. They might be great photographers, amazing accountants or brilliant cleaners, but their numbers are bad and that affects so much of what they do.

This problem is exacerbated when they get busy. A lot of business people look at how busy they are and they think, "I'm doing really well!" However, they've confused being busy with being profitable and the two aren't necessarily the same. And I can tell you that from experience.

Back in 2007 my photography business was taking on a lot of clients, I had multiple photographers working for me and we were really busy. And although we were covering all of our costs, we weren't making a profit. We were all working long hours but our prices weren't high enough.

Like a lot of photographers I was focused on the photography and editing and I didn't take the time to dig into the numbers. Eventually I did and found I had to increase my prices significantly in order to start bringing in a profit. It surprised me when I discovered that our prices needed to be $100 higher than we had been charging all that time.

Athletes know their numbers. As a business owner, do you know your numbers?

We were a bit like amateur athletes, running around a track just for the fun of it, not paying any attention at all to our 'numbers' and therefore not making any improvements to our running.

If you ask any Olympic athlete they'll be able to tell you their numbers. Perhaps it's their personal best performance or the time they think they'll need to win gold or the number of calories they need to consume.

Can you show how much revenue you turned over last week? What was the average dollar value of your sales? Do you know your profit margin as a percentage? Do you have a list showing how many potential clients you've contacted this month?

Do you think it would be helpful if you knew those numbers about your business and were tracking them every week? I know from experience how useful that kind of data is. One of the biggest changes I made in my business was when I finally started tracking all our numbers so I knew exactly what our costs were and how much we were turning over each week.

Once I started doing that consistently I realised we needed to significantly increase our prices. We lost a few clients in the process but the higher fees more than accounted for that and it was one of the best things we ever did. It was scary at the time, of course, but it worked out well for us because we finally knew exactly how well, or in our case, how poorly we were doing when it came to profit margins.

So one thing I think you should do at the end of each week or first thing Monday morning is to go through your numbers, including your sales and expenses and your time spent engaging with clients, and then compare all those numbers with your target.

If you don't know them, including what you actually did and what your target number is, then you won't know what your real costs are and what needs changing, and if you don't change, you will not be the best you can be. If there's one thing we can learn from our Olympian friends it's that we should know our critical numbers.

Your market position determines what you're paid

So what do you do if you find you need to raise your prices?

What you're able to charge comes back to positioning. Your positioning in the market defines where your service stands in relation to others in the marketplace, as well as in the mind of the consumer. For example, when people think of your business do they think of you as the high cost, high quality brand? Are you the one-to-one boutique service brand or are you the large corporate brand? That's your positioning and it's really important.

Before any price rise, a business needs to work on its positioning. I would go so far as to say that it's your positioning, not your ability, that determines what you're paid. Your income and your quality of business life depend more on your positioning than on anything else.

So if you want to move from being the cheap service to being the mid-range or preferably the expensive service, then everything associated with your business has to communicate that same message. For example, you can't be the expensive photographer and have an ugly website. You can't be the expensive photographer and not conduct yourself in a professional manner, including the way you dress. You can't be the expensive photographer and be late to photo shoots.

A price rise is only part of the picture. Everything else you do says either, "It's worth paying this business this much", or it says the opposite.

How do you position yourself the right way?
One thing you can do is make yourself an expert in your market. If people view you as THE guru in whatever it is you do then you can charge a premium price because people assume you can deliver the best result for them.

How do you position yourself as your industry's version of the heart surgeon? You do it with better marketing that includes educational pieces and case studies. You do it by presenting a podcast, by delivering newsletters, by writing blog articles, by interviewing other experts and by charging higher prices.

Yes, charging higher prices in and of itself can help with your positioning, and in turn, that justifies your higher fees. It sounds circular and in a way, it is. However, when you charge more, people assume you must be better at your job than others who charge less, so that can help your positioning in the market.

Create margins in your life

What impact does being a follower of Jesus Christ have upon one's business?

For me, the big difference occurred when I became aware of how much time I was spending in my business and how little time that left me to spend time with my family, to contribute in my community, and to serve and help in my neighbourhood.

When I was working as a photographer I would often be doing twilight photo shoots. They were photography sessions that started before sunset and continued until after sunset. My best work usually occurred at that time simply because that's when the light was absolutely stunning. The pinks and purples in the sky from the setting sun and the lights inside the home, combined with the glow of the moon glistening in the pool, made for stunning marketing images and my clients loved them. And I loved doing them!

However, after finishing the photo shoot I would have to pack up and drive home and in summer this meant I was frequently not home until 8pm or later. My young son would be in bed, often asleep, and I would creep in quietly and look at him there, knowing I didn't have a chance to play outside with him yet again. That would happen day after day after day and it became very difficult.

It came to a head one day during a program the house church I was attending at the time was doing. We were going through a twelve-month study of the teachings of Jesus and what it means to follow Him in practical terms. Each month we would focus on something different and in that particular month we were looking at the importance of creating margins in our life.

The idea of margins was based around the concept of the Sabbath, where God effectively says, "Work well, but one day every week take time out to stop and have a break. Hang out with your friends and enjoy life with your family. Live a little. It's not all about work."

That's what we mean by creating margins. It's about making space in our lives, so that instead of filling them up with activities for every waking minute we actually have a day each week, a Sabbath day, set aside where we are free. If we take that a step further then we can look to create margins not just for a single day but actually adopt a whole of life approach that gives space for us to help others and not be entirely consumed by our businesses.

I know it sounds a little strange to deliberately set time aside, especially for those of us who are entrepreneurs and who like staying busy and completing tasks. Beyond our own internal pressure a lot of us are also being pushed by our boss or our clients or even our church (in terms of attending church meetings and being busy with activities). We've all adopted this attitude that being busy is by definition a good thing, but maybe it's not.

Maybe what we really need isn't more busyness but more

space in our days so we can help our neighbour, we need space in our budgets so that we can give to those who need it, and maybe we need space internally to relax a little and be available, not just for the clients who pay us, but to care for the people around us. Without that availability of time we can't be Jesus when we're really needed.

When we had this discussion in our home church I realised my business structure at the time did not allow me that space in my life. I was filling every working day with shooting and editing photos and I wasn't available to do the things that made life what it ought to be. Perhaps that was partly my fault for not setting clearer expectations with my clients, but I think I was mentally ready to move on and it was then I decided to make a change.

I needed to create more margins in my life so I could better serve my family and actually do the 'love your neighbour' part that Jesus asks of all those who follow Him!

With that in mind, I spent the next six months planning a new business that would give me more margins. I defined what I wanted as the outcome – more flexibility with my time – and I set out to create a business model that would give me that time and allow me to help a friend or neighbour, to play at the park with my son after school, or open up our home and break bread with friends around our table.

With a plan established, we decided to sell our

photography business and when it sold in early 2015, I started my new business in coaching and training photographers. That's what I'm doing today. It keeps me busy and I have a lot to do but I have a lot more time to do things away from work as well.

Every morning before school and (almost) every afternoon, I'm able to play with my son at our local oval or sit down on the lounge room floor with him and play Monopoly. I'm actively involved as vice president at our local junior cricket club and that's something that wouldn't have been possible for me in my old business. Beyond that, I simply have flexibility with my time that allows me to say "yes" to others instead of always needing to say, "I'd love to, but I'm a bit too busy at work at the moment."

For me, the extra freedom I have now that I've deliberately established margins in my life is absolutely beautiful. I feel like I can finally serve the people around me and be a giver who is focused on the external things and not just a busy entrepreneur who is fully committed to the internal things.

If that's something you're able to do, or if you need to change careers or build a new business to give you those margins in your life, I would strongly recommend it. If you can't do that right now, try to make little changes in your life so that you have a little extra space in your calendar, your budget and your own head to make room for life outside of business. It might be one of the best things you ever do.

DARRYL STRINGER

Contributor Profile: Darryl has been an architectural and real estate photographer since 1998. With a lot of persistence he built a very successful business and he is now available to share that knowledge on marketing, pricing and photography with others, making their journey as a photographer a little bit easier.

Self Introduction: A quiet achiever who loves sport, dark chocolate, and thinking outside the box.

Website: www.BuildAPhotographyBusiness.com

Facebook: realestatephotographysystem

Linkedin: Darryl Stringer

Email: darryl@realestatephotographysystem.com

Food for thought

Are there any skills you need to develop or courses you need to do to equip yourself for excellence in your chosen field?

Identify at least two mentors that can help you develop and move forward. These may be someone already working in your industry, a professional coach or even a friend that can help keep you accountable to your goals. Make an appointment with each of them and discuss your goals, dreams, skills and limitations. Commit to an ongoing relationship if you feel this person will help you. If this person doesn't seem to fit well, then find another mentor.

If you're considering starting a business you will need to perform a 'market analysis'. This is an important step because it will identify your competitors, establish the need for your business and therefore the likely number of customers or clients and help you determine your pricing in relation to other businesses in the same field. Your analysis may show that you will need to promote your business to a wider demographic or areas than you previously thought in order to meet costing and profit expectations.

Develop an 'action plan' that will guide you through each step in getting your business up and running. List everything you need to do and decide in what order they need to be done. This same process can be used if you are changing direction with your business, developing new marketing strategies or looking to enlarge your business in some way.

Perform a 'break even cost analysis' and 'return on investment analysis' for your business or proposed business. If you aren't sure where to start, talk to an accountant. Your bank will also be able to assist you in the early stages, especially if you are setting up business bank accounts. Otherwise, there is a mountain of information on the internet.

What do you want your business to 'look like'? How will you present yourself and your business to the public to ensure your business is seen as professional eg. Will your staff need uniforms?

What days and times will you set aside for family, friends, church, relaxation, sport, study, etc? Block these out in your diary before you start setting schedules and appointments.

Chapter Five
Declutter Your Life

For this season in my life, God is calling me to be a minister of the gospel through serving people as a professional organiser.

If you've ever struggled when you hear "your workplace is your ministry", then you're not alone. What does it even mean when we say things like "equip the saints for ministry" or "you're called to be Jesus to your colleagues"? Are these just things Christians say, but don't really mean?

I hope that my unique position as both an entrepreneur and church leader will enable me to share my journey, both practically and experientially.

The conception of my business, 'Simply Organised', story started about 30 years ago, when I was entering primary school. School was perfect for me – it was organised, structured and we were encouraged to be neat in the work we produced. I quickly learnt that my bent in school was toward efficiency rather than perfection. If I could finish a project and have time left at the end and still receive a high mark I was thrilled.

This became particularly evident in senior school where while doing my last two years of high school I also enjoyed a busy extracurricular schedule. I was the music captain, the sports house captain, on the debating team, part of Amnesty International, a member of our church youth group, playing in the school jazz band, taking private piano lessons, singing in the school choir, part of the school musical, working in a part time job and I had a social life to boot. At our year twelve valedictory dinner I was presented with the award for the busiest student in that year level.

As life got busier I discovered that being organised was also saving me time, money and headspace!

Multitasking and finding efficient ways to do simple tasks became second nature to me. Organising and decluttering followed naturally as I married, moved out of home and started my own family. I was running our busy church office at twenty-one and realised that my organisational skills weren't something that everyone had. I've always enjoyed feeling organised but as life got busier I discovered that it was also saving me time, money and headspace and I loved helping other people be more efficient and productive. I had several roles as a personal assistant to managers in not-for-profit organisations and the satisfaction of helping organise someone else's time and schedule was incredibly rewarding.

Fast forward to today and I enjoy working with beautiful women around the country doing something I'm passionate about. I get the privilege of helping women to declutter and organise their homes. As well as totally loving my business, I also feel strongly that it is the place where God would have me serve Him in this season of life.

I love what Martin Luther said about service to God:

> "The idea that service to God should have only to do with a church altar, singing, reading, sacrifice and the like is without doubt but the worst trick of the devil. How could the devil have led us more effectively astray than by the narrow conception that the service of God takes place only in the church and by works done therein... the whole world could abound with services to the Lord... not only in churches but also in the home, kitchen, workshop and field."

Ministry is how we bring the kingdom of God to earth. Jesus prayed, "Your kingdom come, Your will be done, on earth as it is in heaven." So whether we are the CEO of a bank or founder of a small start-up, we can use our businesses to be a vehicle of God's love to the world.

Finding true freedom

I first read the book of Ecclesiastes cover to cover when I was about nineteen and instantly fell in love with the teachings of King Solomon. Life is fleeting and success is here today, but gone tomorrow. So what if I could help people clear the clutter and enable them to focus on the important things in life? I saw that excess was building up astronomically in our lives – not only physically in our homes, but mentally and emotionally and as humans we just can't focus when we're surrounded by too much stuff. Most people don't know it until they experience it, but when we're surrounded by clutter, our relationships, creativity and spiritual growth are hindered.

Jesus said that what we do for those deemed 'least' in our world, we do for Him!

What a great gift I can give to people to not only help them clear tangible clutter, but also enable them to experience physical, emotional and spiritual freedom as a result. Jesus said that what we do for those deemed 'least' in our world, we do for Him. In my field that means I get to work closely alongside those ridden with shame, guilt, embarrassment, social isolation, judgement and self-loathing. My everyday interaction with clients gives me ample opportunity to show unconditional love to people and speak to their true worth; not the value they have tried to attain through their physical possessions.

Genuine relationships with my clients is what makes my business so enjoyable. Not only do I love physically clearing clutter and the great results that brings, but through those relationships I am sometimes granted the opportunity to share my faith with them. I wanted to write 'often' granted the opportunity, but the reality is it's not often. It's sometimes. I hope and pray it increases, but my job isn't to manufacture the opportunity, it is to be prepared with an answer for the hope that I have, whenever I am asked (1 Peter 3:15).

Godly Business Values

As well as having opportunity to show the love of Jesus to people through business, how someone conducts themselves and the values they display are of vital importance. For me, the key is this: do you display Godly values in business because they're good for business or because they're Godly? It may seem like one and the same thing, but my challenge is: Will you stick to your Godly values even when it's bad for business?

For instance, honesty. I was recently contacted by a wealthy client who wanted to book me to help her do some decluttering. After seeing her immaculate house I was honest and told her I didn't think she needed my services as she seemed to already be keeping a beautiful home. I knew that my honesty was probably going to cost me thousands of dollars, but I had the integrity to say it anyway. Interestingly, she explained that although she felt confident to declutter on her own, she was after the company and expert experience that would make the whole process much quicker and so she went ahead with the booking. Our honest conversation made our business transaction a memorable one and reinforced to me that being a Christian entrepreneur requires we see past the dollar signs to our greater purpose.

A Foot in Both Camps

What I haven't mentioned yet is that, as well as being a business owner and entrepreneur, my husband and I also pastor a church. Talk about having a foot in both camps!

I love it. I love that God knows me well enough to allow me the freedom to pursue my dreams both inside and outside of the church. My husband has pastored at three different churches during our fifteen year marriage and I've loved serving alongside him in every place. I have held positions on executive leaderships and boards as well as run youth groups, life groups, evangelism teams, Sunday service teams and been involved in children's ministry.

Fear is not the best motivator for any business decision!

The tug and pull of 'ministry' vs 'business' is familiar to me and I still dance with it at times. For me the opposition has never been external, it has always been an internal battle. Is church ministry a higher calling than business? Is business more holy when it makes loads of money to give to the poor? How do you know if you're being successful in business if you're not seeing clients or customers become Christians? I think as I've matured, the line between sacred and secular has not only blurred but is slowly being erased. My service to God is my wholehearted, unrestrained, passionate love for Him and for people. *"To love the Lord my God with all my heart, with all my soul and with all my mind."* (Matt 22:37)

At one stage I justified making money through my business by deciding I was going to give 100% of my profits away. This wasn't something I had heard from God about. It was more of a fear reaction to financial success. Now there are a lot of businesses run by Christians who do operate in a not-for-profit set up, but I'd suggest fear of success isn't the best motivator for that business decision!

A Child Entrepreneur

I started my first business at the tender age of eight and have rarely had a season in life that didn't include some kind of entrepreneurial adventure. Even as a child, if a business idea didn't succeed as planned, I just picked up my creative ideas, learnt from the experience and tried my hand at something new. A lot of my endeavours were philanthropic in nature and brought me much joy. I have always held the belief that there is boundless money and resources in the world, we just need to provide people opportunities to get involved in good causes.

A couple of years ago, my own two boys, who were seven and nine years old at the time, worked tirelessly making jewellery to sell, with the vision of helping to provide clean drinking water to a remote community. They ended up making so much money the Herald Sun printed an article on their business and their global impact. I'm delighted to see my own two boys actively looking for ways to better the world around them.

Every season has a lesson!

'Simply Organised' is by far my most successful company to date, but I've learnt so many valuable lessons along the way. What I do today is a result of years of learning about myself and my passions. I have a real desire to make a significant difference in our world during my lifetime. I have a vision to run a successful company that has capacity to grow and change as required. I desire to reflect Jesus to my staff, my clients, the media and all I come into contact with.

I desperately want to show people that consumerism isn't the path to happiness and that you are worth more than the sum of your possessions. I want to wake up each day and go to a job I enjoy. I desire the flexibility to serve both my family and my business as needed. Ultimately I want to finish not just my life, but each season along the way and hear the words, *"Well done, good and faithful servant."*

Seasons of Life

- For this current season in my life, God is calling me to be a minister of the gospel through serving people as a professional organiser.

- For another season in my life, God called me to be a minister of the gospel through serving my children as a stay at home mum.

- For another season in my life, God called me to be a minister of the gospel through starting and then selling, a children's party supply business.

- For another season in my life, God called me to be a minister of the gospel through serving high school students as a youth pastor.

- For another season in my life, God called me to be a minister of the gospel through being the treasurer of the school fundraising committee.

- For another season in my life, God called me to be a minister of the gospel through nursing a sick child back to health.

Can you see how no matter our season, whether in business or in family, our purpose is still the same? No matter which season you're in now, whether prosperous or frustrating, visible or hidden, you are still called to be a minister of the gospel.

Confidence & Humility

A question I've asked myself quite a bit over the last twelve months is how do I balance confidence and humility in my company and in my day to day work with clients? How does being a Christian entrepreneur in this regard set me apart? I find the line between confidence and arrogance can be a fine one and is there even space for humility when you're setting out to be the best in your industry? I'm naturally a very confident person, I know my strengths and my weaknesses and I believe in myself to adapt to new situations with wisdom and success. But how do we still remain humble? How do we not make the ever so subtle slide from confidence to arrogance?

> **Confidence is evidence based rather than ego based.**

My clients are often looking for reassurance when they're chatting to me about potentially working together in their homes. They usually ring at a point of desperation and are nervous on the phone that their home will be the most cluttered I've ever seen and I won't be able to help them. I used to feel arrogant saying to them, "I'm really good at what I do and I know you'll be glad we worked together." But I've learnt that confidence is evidence based rather than ego based. My confidence is in my skills. I am good at what I do and I've honed my abilities through practice, education and hard work. *(Side note: if you're not actually awesome at what you do, don't claim to be. Instead work hard to develop your skills so that your confidence is based on reality and not just a dream.)*

I've got a little saying: 'Love what you do and be awesome at it.' It's the amazing power of passion and ability working together than can give you legitimate confidence.

Confidence is magnetic for clients; as consumers we are drawn to confidence and feed off the confidence of others. And the awesome thing about confidence is that it increases the expectations of clients and with increased expectation the whole atmosphere can change.

When I work with a client with high expectations, not only do I rise to the occasion, but they bring an expectant energy to the session and are more likely to come away having experienced not just a less cluttered and more organised home, but having had some personal breakthrough along the way. For me, during a session with a client, I need for their nervous energy to be absorbed by my confidence so they have the space to be dealing with the 'why' behind their clutter. It's never just about the stuff itself – there is always a journey to how they came to be feeling overwhelmed and stressed in their own home.

I trust God to bring the right clients at the right time!

If I lacked the confidence that I can help anyone no matter how cluttered their house is, then the client would spend the whole session worried and trying to appease me. Instead I want them to feel peace, calm and supported so as well as decluttering physically there is space for some self-reflection and personal growth.

My confidence also comes from knowing that it is God's will for me to run my business and offer the services I do. I trust Him to bring the right clients at the right time and to lead me as I make decisions and work alongside women in their homes. And the humility that balances out the confidence is knowing it is God's grace that allows me to do what I love.

Only a couple of years ago, about 18 months into starting my company, I became very sick with glandular fever. I was completely bed ridden for about five months, unable to work at all and wondered if this was the end of 'Simply Organised'. But as I recovered, God provided the right clients at exactly the right times and gave me the grace and strength for each session. A great gift from God has been the ability to not stress when it seems like I'm having a slow client week, I have a deep trust that God knows what I need way better than I know myself.

I believe when we get the balance of true confidence and humility right, it is a powerful combination for our businesses. I also believe outside of God, this balance is impossible to master.

Decluttering in the Bible
I talked before about ministry being about bringing the kingdom of God to earth and I believe it's important for me as a business owner to not only conduct my business as a Christian and interact with people in a way that reflects the heart of Jesus but also that my actual work reflects the values of the kingdom.

The problem is that the word 'decluttering' doesn't appear even once in the Bible. Is the problem of clutter and the solution of decluttering that has taken the world by storm, a new concept? Look a little deeper into the Bible with me and discover what God has been saying about clutter for thousands of years.

If you want a one stop chapter in the Bible where Jesus addresses the issues of clutter, possessions and worry, flick to the twelfth chapter of Luke. Read the whole chapter then examine your heart for where clutter has distracted you from the important things in life.

In Luke 12:16 we have the account where Jesus talks about a rich man who finds comfort in the fact that he can tear down his current barns to build bigger ones to store all his wheat and other goods for the future. Sound familiar? How many people do you know who have purchased bigger houses because their old house isn't big enough for all their stuff? Jesus then says exactly what the rich man needs to hear, and indeed our whole culture today: *"A person is a fool to store up earthly wealth but not have a rich relationship with God."*

Our value is much more than the sum of our earthly possessions!

Too many possessions and an excess of 'stuff' distract us from the important things in life. You may feel that your level of possessions is normal and not distracting at all but I challenge you to walk around your home with fresh eyes and see the items that you no longer need, no longer love or no longer use.

Luke 12:22 then goes on to a conversation Jesus has with his disciples. I've heard this passage taught on from the perspective of worry; that we need not worry as God will provide all our needs. However, look at Jesus' words in regards to earthly possessions. The accumulation and comfort of stuff isn't going to reduce your worry. I find that many clients keep unnecessary items in their home 'just in case', like a security blanket. A crippling, overwhelming security blanket of clutter that promises security, but never delivers. They worry what will happen if they let go of things they've held onto for years. And like a double edged sword, the words of Jesus ring true throughout history – *"Wherever your treasure is, there the desires of your heart will be also."*

Read the writings of King Solomon, the richest man to ever live and yet he arrives at the conclusion that it's *"all meaningless, a chasing after the wind"* as earthly possessions do nothing to satisfy the deep cries of his heart.

Or Paul, a man from great stature in Jewish society, finds his greatest satisfaction and joy in life being imprisoned for the sake of Jesus. He goes from having it all, to having nothing and can still pen the words, *"To live is Christ but to die is gain"*.

These and many other scriptures encourage me in my work as a professional organiser. Sometimes it is only when the excess is removed from our lives that the deep desires of our heart can be finally heard. And once they're heard and we have removed the clutter we can hear the voice of God more clearly and deepen our relationship with Him. My clients describe it like this: *"it's like a weight has been lifted from my shoulders"* or *"I feel like a fog has been lifted and I can finally see clearly again"*.

The act of decluttering, although being predominantly physical, is also a great spiritual discipline!

Decluttering is the removal of anything that hinders or weighs us down or distracts us from fixing our eyes on Jesus (Hebrews 12:1). With decluttering comes many other benefits: time is regained from shopping and looking after our things, our minds become clearer and less distracted, our finances are freed up and kingdom investment is possible.

So I'm not just in the business of organising things into baskets and tidying up. I'm in the business of life change. I love that my ministry and my call and my passion are to build my business and help people live a more simple life. I no longer shy away from financial success because I see the great power for good that strong businesses can make.

For this season in my life, God is calling me to be a minister of the gospel through serving people as a professional organiser. And I love it!

AMY REVELL

Declutter Queen and Professional Organiser

Contributor Profile: Amy Revell is an author, podcaster, blogger and professional organiser. Amy has always been a super organised person and this natural gift has developed into a successful business helping women find freedom through decluttering and organising their homes.

Self Introduction: The Declutter Queen and minimalist who loves an organising project and drinking tea with friends.

Author of 'Simply Organised': http://simplyorganised.net/book

Website: www.simplyorganised.net

Facebook: simplyorganisedPO

Linkedin: Amy Revell

Instagram: simply.organised

Email: amy.revell@simplyorganised.net

Food for thought

List your most natural talents, skills and abilities. List your experiences, both life experience and work experience. How are these being used in your business or life? How can they be used?

Do you display Godly values in your business? Are there any areas where adjustment may be needed so that your business values and your personal Christian values are aligned?

Do you see your business as a money-making venture or a ministry to a group of people? What is your 'why'?

How do you determine how much of your profit is given to God, other ministries and charities? Do you tithe on your income? Do you believe in tithing? Do you just give a set amount each week/month or do you wait on God for His leading? 'We are blessed, so we can be a blessing'. God is generous and we are called to be a generous people. 'Give and it will be given unto you'.

What season of life do you feel you are in right now? What is the lesson you need to learn or the truth you need to glean from this season?

Where does your confidence come from? Do you lack confidence?

Look back at your skills, talents, abilities and experience. Where have you been successful before? Doing these things in your own business is not very much different to doing them for someone else. If you have been successful before you can be successful now and that's where your confidence comes from.

Do you believe that God has led you to be in business? Is God a partner in your business?

How can you include God more in your business?

Chapter Six
The Salt of The Earth

Are you playing small from fear?

I clearly see my work as my ministry and always have and that is where I spend most of my time. I'm not overly involved in any functions at any churches I have been a part of and some churches just don't accept that in me. I believe God is much bigger than just a church community and over and over again He has shown me how much I have helped others who don't go near a church.

Some say I should be leading Bible studies or going to women's church groups because I am such a teacher and community builder but that is not my calling. Some churches have told me my work at times interferes with church activities. I need to be available to do church stuff and my work is just a way to make money. **What?**

God is my planning person

For me, the idea of my work just making money couldn't be further from the truth. For years, I was a passionate Management Consultant led by God. Sometimes in my own business, other times working for consulting firms.

Before commencing every project or piece of work, I would first pray about it and ask God to guide and show me the best way to solve the client's dilemma. I would run leadership programs, coach managers and lead strategic planning workshops for executive groups. With every single project I knew God went before me and showed me what I needed to do in that particular situation.

Of course, I planned and created resources and developed running sheets and email follow ups for any programs or work I did but I often found that God would give me a hint or a nudge to add something to what I was going to teach or coach. Sometimes it was just five minutes before walking into the room but it was ALWAYS some of the best insights that people said were so helpful.

People pick up that we have an energy of love and support!

No, it was not me sharing Jesus. And no, I was not leading a Bible study. But you know what happened over and over again? Executives and managers that I worked with would often say, *"There's something different about you. You really care about us. You are super competent and give us more than we have requested in whatever issue we have asked for but you work side by side with us. You really listen and help us find our solution and then teach us how to do it on our own. So many consultants don't do that because they want to keep coming back so they can keep charging us. You are very different and actually coach us to be sure that we can follow the path on our own and even further to make it better."*

I see that whole picture as a God picture. When I would pull up to a project I would say a prayer in my car. Some projects were a big challenge and I needed real guidance to know how to best approach them. And God amazingly gave it to me. No, I did not share Jesus or talk about the Bible. I felt my calling was to live from God's wisdom and leading inside me. Enjoying life, being honest about challenges and fully supporting my clients.

I took business trips to the United States and many to my beloved country of Qatar and what was I on about? I was doing the work I enjoyed doing, expressing gratitude and building authentic relationships with the diverse group of people there. When I came back to Australia the first time I went there, one woman at church said to me, "So did you evangelise the Muslims? I'm thinking of going over there to evangelise them?" My big answer was "NO WAY!". It is about being authentic, getting to know people, having genuine conversations and being of service to them in my professional role.

I believe we should be salt of the earth. Salt is imperceptible, but adds great flavour and that is what I believe is my contribution. I teach students who are Hindu, Muslim, Christian and many other faiths and to me, being salt of the earth is living with God inside me and reflecting His presence through me as I go about each day. I make mistakes and do things wrong at times but it all makes me human and much more relatable to others. As I focus on God and ask Him what I should be led to do, I get my next steps and go further and further. And I've lost count of the number of times people of all faiths tell me they really feel a sense of God in me. And I then get to share who my God is.

When God is in you and you just live – people know!

As salt of the earth, we should be tasty to people and have them know that there is something wonderfully different about us so they want to know more. That has happened to me over and over again as I just live with God's indwelling presence inside me, instead of wearing some kind of outer coat that makes me feel like I must tell people about God and try to pressure them to listen to Him. Of course, this does not work.

Your work does not have to be lined up with church ministry – be authentic.

Some people work on oil rigs. Others are graphic artists. Some are teachers. Some are council workers. In essence in every field there are Christian workers. And to me it is about doing the best job and relating to people in service of what you do – and doing it naturally.

So what am I saying here? Be YOU. Have fun. Know that when God is in you, you can fully enjoy life and share experiences with people. Let people tell you about their lives and their challenges, let them tell you their story. Listen! Don't become negative about it, ask them how they'd like to be. Often they are looking for answers but as salt of the earth, I find that I can share the right amount of salt for the occasion. I don't pull out the four spiritual laws and lead them to being a Christian. I ask them about their faith, what they do in life and at work, then in that context, I can tell them about my experiences.

If God opens a door and some people put you down, follow God anyway!

Sometimes God opens doors for you that some people do not understand. God led me to talk about the Law of

Attraction in a way that drew some Christians to God. I believe that the whole universe and energetic field have been created by God. And that as we pray (put our thoughts out to God) we are given guidance and leading.

Some said to me, "Oh my, you are really going to the dark side", and I knew that was not the case at all. God clearly guided me to know which ones were dark side discussions and I did not participate in those. As I prayed and visualised what I believed God was leading me to do, I slowly felt nudges of taking the next step. I always felt love and grace as I shared.

So when I started to speak to groups, I found there were many who had turned away from churches because they were so strict with lots of rules that really did not necessarily follow what God was doing. So, as I spoke about the Law of Attraction, I always started by saying "I call it God because God created the energetic field and it is one of the ways we receive answered prayers.

But if you find it difficult to call it 'God' just call it 'Universe' and think of the spiritual dimension in your life." Every time I spoke, at least two or three Christians would come up to me afterward telling me that my 'God-type scenario' was one they could relate to and it gave them a desire to come back to God instead of just putting it all aside.

The joy of the Lord renews our strength.
God's Spirit in us should bring us joy, jobs, experiences, relationships and more in a fulfilling, happy way. So what does that show to others? That we are doing just what we love and we are also enjoying it even though it is hard work.

I don't know about you, but if I find that I am aiming for a certain situation or job and it doesn't come through, I know that it means God has something even better waiting for me. Sometimes the job or experience turns out to be different to what I actually thought it would be. There are so many who don't know God who get fully discouraged and insecure about things that don't work out.

Discouragement is part of life.
Yes, of course we all have times when we are down or discouraged. That is life. But as Christians, after we experience a short time of feeling discouraged, we know it is time to turn back to God and see what He is showing us next.

Some of us have health issues, some of us are in problematic marriages or have a mother-in-law who is difficult to get along with or work for managers who cause us a lot of stress or grief. All of these things are challenges. The Christian life is not just one big 'oh yes God, I'll just follow you'. The experiences and challenges of life should motivate us to turn to God where we can find direction for the next step or guidance on how we can move ahead and have a better experience as we change our thoughts or views or actions to start improving our situation.

Live and love boldly!
I say live boldly. Really dig into what you LOVE doing and work on how you can make it happen. And it does not have to be 'ministry' or something 'Christian'. You may just LOVE teaching fitness. Or just LOVE doing marketing. Or LOVE working in a bank. Follow your heart and listen to

the guidance that God is giving you and remember that what He is leading you to, is supposed to be fun, fulfilling and something that you really enjoy doing.

If you are in a challenging situation now, think about who you can talk to, to find another perspective. If a thought crosses your mind to call a certain person, do it, because they may be the very person who will show you the next step or guide you to see what needs to change so your situation can start to improve.

As Christians, we have a sense of guidance, trust and ability to go well beyond what we think is possible because God goes before us!

I have dozens and dozens of stories about how God opened doors for me when I thought there might be no way possible. And as those doors opened, they revealed much more than I ever thought they would. It's not just one big happy life even with God, but as Christians, no matter what we face, we have a sense of guidance, trust and ability to go well beyond what we think is possible because God goes before us.

Our God is a big God, He doesn't play small. Are you? Don't let fear stop you. Listen to your heart and take one step in the direction you feel led to go. You'll find God will guide you on your path. Sometimes it is a challenge and there are bumps in the road but if you keep following the path that feels right, things will unfold in the right time. And it will be amazing!

LINDA CHAOUSIS

Contributor Profile: Linda wears a lot of hats. A writer. A speaker. A podcaster. A wellness advocate. And yet, every one of these has a common passionate thread of hers going through it: to encourage people to follow their path even if others say "why would you do that?".

Self Introduction: Her favourite place is any beach, at times with her dogs and a good hot latte. Oh yeah!

Website: www.lindachaousis.com

Facebook: thinkitbelieveitcreateit

Linkedin: Linda Chaousis

Email: linda@lindachaousis.com

Food for thought

Identify any fears in your life, either about yourself, your family, your future or your business.

What do you need to do to overcome them?

How does your church view your business activities, in a positive or negative way?

How does their viewpoint affect you? Does anything in your mindset need to change in relation to their rejection or acceptance?

Have you shared a business idea or proposal to someone who has put you down or given a negative response? How did this make you feel? What have you done to overcome any negativity?

Is your current business or employment bringing you joy, work, experiences and relationships in a fulfilling and happy way? If not, find out why. God may be leading you to something new.

Discouragement is a normal part of life. How do you deal with discouragement?

What is the one thing that you love doing? Is God leading you to develop a business in this field?

If you are in a challenging situation right now, who can you talk to for reassurance and guidance?

Chapter Seven
Better, not Bigger

Twenty years, ten months and twenty seven days ago (at the time of writing), I looked up into a star filled night sky and I was overcome by feelings of regret, fear, loss and embarrassment.

Eight years earlier I had graduated from one of the most prestigious and expensive schools in Australia, 'The King's School', won a national swimming title and was the 'golden child' in the eyes of my family and friends. Aside from average academic ability I had a choice of any career I wanted.

However, by my twenty fifth birthday I had dropped out, failed university, burnt countless relationships, partied way too hard, had more casual jobs than I could remember and was living week to week often borrowing from family and friends till my next pay.

I didn't like where I was, what I had become and what the future would hold if I was to continue down the same path I was on. I also remember thinking massive change only comes from massive action.

Reassessment and commitment

I won't bore you with the emotional details, however on my twenty fifth birthday I decided to commit to a savings plan of $100 per month. I soon calculated that this would never be enough to be rich or 'financially free', so I reassessed and upped my savings to my maximum possible commitment of $250 per week, which at that time was about 60% of my income. I also defined how much investment income I wanted in order to be 'financially free'. Back in 1996 this was $50,000 per year.

By my projections I estimated this would require $1,000,000 of investments and a commitment of twenty two years to achieve my 'financial independence' (based on a 10% p.a. net return and drawing down a 5% of this balance after reaching it).

At first, saving 60% of my income was horrible. I had to change my priorities and attitude. In hindsight my drive probably came from my desire to punish myself for my earlier shortcomings, prove to myself that I wasn't a failure and to feel some sense of worth when I was around others.

After three months, my motivation was less emotional. I had trained myself to do more with less and at the same time started to relish this new commitment in a similar way I had previously when training in the pool for my swimming. I also realised the only control I had was my savings amount and my regularity i.e. my goal will be achieved as long as I simply do the work.

With greater confidence came higher goals. I decided to set myself a stretch goal of $15,000 saved by the end of twelve months with my reward being any money saved above this, I could spend however I wanted. With this as my incentive, I took on extra shifts and threw myself into learning more about investments and finances.

After achieving my first year of savings I met with a financial adviser. It was a bit daunting and scary and I can't really remember much more than he had a nice office, seemed like a nice person but didn't want much to do with me because I was more an accumulator (regular saver) rather than a lump sum investor.

Time for a career change

Two years later at twenty seven, I applied for a career change and successfully attained a position as a bank teller. Part of the bank teller internship was to meet with a bank adviser. Up until this meeting I was still at a loss as to my true career path, however post this meeting I remember thinking that my professional calling is to be a financial adviser. I can learn about money, I can help people have more choice and certainty in their own lives and I would be paid to help them. What a fantastic career.

From there I enrolled to the Securities Institute (SIA), applied for all internal training, joined professional associations and applied all I was learning into my own financial situation. I resigned from the bank in 2001 and worked with an independent advisory business whilst continuing further studies and obtaining my Financial Planning Certification in 2004. Since then I have operated my own business and continue to educate myself via trusted mentors, having my own financial adviser and surrounding myself with a team of the best in class specialists across the different areas of money management.

More than making a commitment, I found that it's the doing that moves you forward. This 'doing' gave me a fresh focus in life and self confidence that had gone M.I.A. between finishing school and my twenty fifth birthday. It also opened doors of opportunity for me, transitioning from casual bar worker, to bank teller then financial adviser and onto establishing my own boutique financial planning business.

Thank God for that bus

I believe we are given signs in life. In fact, I literally saw mine walking to work. 'Better, Not Bigger' flashed before me as a bus turned the corner and sped off. Since then this simple message has changed my perspective of life to its core. It has rippled through my business dealings, relationships, health, experiences, goals and beliefs. It has helped me to reveal the more authentic me.

'KISS', an acronym for 'Keep it simple, stupid', was created in 1960 as a design principle used by the U.S. Navy. This 'KISS' principle states that most systems work best if they are kept simple rather than made complicated; therefore simplicity should be a key goal in design and unnecessary complexity should be avoided. In fact, I believe simplicity embodies elegance, wisdom, effectiveness and profitability.

I think I'm in good company here: Leonardo da Vinci stated, "Simplicity is the ultimate sophistication". Albert Einstein declared, "The definition of genius is taking the complex and making it simple".

While de-cluttering is the first step to simplifying our lives, stopping here cheats us of the greater benefits simplicity has to offer. Furthermore, by rebuilding something new from less, that new thing will be of superior quality and will be more liberating, empowering and inspirational.

So while the saying 'live more, with less' may sound like a paradox; the truth is, our very own human genetic design i.e. our DNA, is coded to identify, adapt and evolve to be more efficient for us to better survive.

Time for a review

I recently benchmarked my progress of applying this 'KISS' principle to my 'Better, Not Bigger' edict, in my financial planning business. The review revealed both some expected and refreshing results. Most importantly clients told me they, "feel supported and more confident than previously and are on track to achieving their goals".

I have also seen an increase in new client enquiries and increased bottom line profitability. This has been reassuring feedback from the people who pay our bills that being 'Better, not bigger' is a good business model for both them and us. These results speak for themselves and are proof that truly living the 'Keep it simple' and 'Better, not bigger' principles is an elegant, wise, effective and profitable business and life model. However, the internal effects have been even more nothing short of life changing.

Profound benefits I discovered by simplifying my life:

- **Clarity**
When you know what's important to you and you are making choices aligned to your core values, decisions are easy. From this place we can better filter our choices between what will help us, what will hinder us or what may harm us. This is very different from having a life full of complexity that leads to reactionary and emotional decision making. Our reactions set off a chain of events that affect others around us. Responding appropriately more often leads to a problem being resolved rather than becoming bigger.

- **Peace**
Defined as freedom from disturbance and a time where there is no war or war has ended. Rather than chasing after things that are important to others, peace allows us

to focus on what's important to us. As we eliminate our distractions, we can use our time more wisely and achieve our goals sooner. Keeping my objectives simple, gives me the peace to focus on my clients more and continually find fresh ways to deliver even better value to them.

- **Health**

We all know what we need to do to live a healthy life, so it's wise not to delay this. The less sedentary we are, the less fat and junk food we consume and the more we hydrate with water. Ninety nine percent of the time improved health starts simply with getting outside and going for a walk. Consider the domino effect that exercising more, eating better, hydrating more, having more energy, feeling less stressed and enjoying life more would have on your relationships (including yourself) and your decision making.

- **Relationships**

What we feel on the inside we express on the outside. Under anger is hurt, under hurt is fear, under fear is vulnerability. Vulnerability is the fertile soil where love, peace and growth is best developed. Being in a relationship where you can be vulnerable without fear brings a deep peace. When you remove the distractions, over-reactions and peer pressures and make time to talk and reflect, it enables you to deepen your relationships and build a foundation of trust.

- **Confidence**

Less distractions coupled with my choices aligned to my core values buoys my confidence. This has not only sped up my decision making process it has also held me back from making poor decisions. I have learnt to let go of what I can't control and focus on what I can control.

- **Liberation**
By living the 'KISS' and 'Better, not bigger' principles, I have developed greater emotional, intellectual and physical agility. Today I have increased motivation to do more of the things that only I can do and I receive a direct benefit from these simple choices. These include diving on the Great Barrier Reef, exercising, bush walking, quality time with friends & family, developing my authentic self and embracing new experiences.

- **Gratitude**
Living with less gives a greater understanding of necessity and a deeper appreciation of what is a luxury. Being grateful for real relationships, deep friendships, good health and honesty keeps me from being distracted by the bling, the ego and the noise.

Consideration of the difficulties that others face and being able to help where I can is both humbling and reassuring. I boast less and I am deeply thankful for the opportunities and position I have been given to help others live a more fulfilling life.

Embracing a 'Keep It Simple' edict isn't easy and the majority of people will move on to something new and shiny, however, the results I have discovered from my 'Keep It Simple' and 'Better, Not Bigger' mandates has been profound, rewarding and valuable.

The battle of self-talk

"Why bother? Why struggle and strive? In the end, one is not getting out of here alive. More than this, in maybe three and definitely four generations, no one will know or remember us anyway, aside from maybe some old pictures, certificates and titles. Who am I living life for? Myself or the good opinion of others?

Invisible bars of expectation and limiting beliefs imprison me from experiencing who I truly am and could become, not only for myself but in my relationships with others. The struggle to accumulate wealth and the approval of others leaves me burnt out and cynical. Full of worries and looking forward to embracing death, where dashed hopes and worries would haunt me no longer.

Step out in front of that car, jump off that balcony or maybe a quick slash with a sharp knife. It's so easy to be one moment alive and the next, not!"

I remember this self-talk starting back in 2010 and carrying on at least up to mid-2014. Looking back on these dark years, I was truly broken by my own doing and I believe, by the will of God. My memory scars continue to heal today, however at that time back in 2014, I first needed to make a huge leap into the unknown.

I felt lost and confused, angry with myself and God and feeling abandoned, shameful, hurt and estranged from the pleasures of life. I considered my only remaining option and began my process of making peace with God (the Creator of all life). I remember many times breaking down and crying on this journey of disarmament, acknowledgement and acceptance.

We need God, for both our peace and as an enabler for us to experience a higher quality of life!

The reason I share this with you is to encourage you and remind you that to be alive is to feel pain, sorrow and fear. However, if we are to feel truly alive, peace must be our foundation. The fact is God doesn't need us, but we need God, for both our own peace and as an enabler for us to experience a higher quality of life.

Regardless of what happens in my future, peace is my constant goal for myself and others. I would not be where I am today without the experience of those dark years, nor would I be as at peace with myself and life as I am now.

In mid-2014 an opportunity to do what I love in a location that inspires me every single day presented itself. The challenge involved a life changing transition, including but not limited to, a change of office, new clients, transitioning existing clients, new licences, large sums of money to be borrowed and the unknown.

The place was Cairns, Australia and I embraced the chance to do the one thing I love to do: help people live their ideal life without financial stress, to have peace without worries.

Change is never easy however finding peace and making choices aligned to what is important to me made my decision all that much easier. So with this confidence I stepped forward into the unknown, without any guarantees and holding true to my faith and core values.

If not now, then when?

We meet again my old friend! It has been twenty eight years since we last greeted each other. I am here, not to compete with you or anyone else, I'm here only to enjoy the experience and improve myself. It's 5.30am, my toes grip the ledge of the swimming pool as I roll forward and dive into the water.

These days my private competition pool may be less than fifty meters walk away from my home, surrounded by coconut palms, with the water a comfortable twenty five degrees, however I still need to make a conscious decision to get in and swim!

Be it diving into a pool half asleep at 5.30am or wanting to achieve anything important to me in life, after committing myself, I have always experienced an initial shock, then awareness and the reality of my decision, followed by my acceptance and then simply getting on with the job or task at hand.

Regardless of how many books I read or courses I complete, for me success has required full immersion, simply doing the work and improving my technique and strengths along the way. Just like learning to swim, to become confident and competent required me to step out of my comfort zone and into the pool.

The danger is that success (earned or not) is highly euphoric as it releases natural dopamines within you. The quest for this natural high can become all-consuming if left unchecked.

Committing and following through on our own personal expectations is self-empowering!

An even greater danger is when the expectations of success are **not** realised. A sense of failure can increase our risk of depression and/or seeking external gratification in order to self-validate. I have experienced both, in and out of the pool.

Swimming has taught me a lot about myself and life. And while we love to test ourselves against others and everyone loves a winner but the real winner is the individual participant. Why? Because simply committing and following through on our own personal expectations is self-empowering. Getting out of a warm comfortable bed and into a cold wet pool is character building.

Appreciating that while others may be more naturally gifted, have the newest equipment or simply be better, in most cases everyone can enjoy the experience of self-improvement i.e. learning to swim. Doing the work is both meditative and a proven path for improvement. Most advances in life often happen after a long plateau but as we push through and pursue our goals, our character is developed and breakthrough comes.

And finally as with anything in life, to be your best you need to be committed and have committed people around you. Both those who love you and those you pay to help you improve. Accountability is the motivation to action.

Here are some tips I apply in my own life:

- Be good to those who support you. If you don't, success will be even harder than it already is.
- Do or Do Not. There is no Try. *(Yoda –Star Wars)*
- Commit to personal expectations that impress you, not expectations you think will impress others or to fulfill expectations from others.
- Remain committed to your passion, purpose and values. Doing so provides greater clarity and commitment and heightens the possibility of success.

- Know how much is your 'enough'. The purpose of work is to create, the purpose of money is to have enough to fund your purpose.

- The past is dry cement. Don't let success get to your head and let go of your failures.

- Be happy with the plateau, knowing that doing the work and perseverance will bring you closer to a spike in improvement.

- Whatever you want to be, become or achieve in life, at some point you are going to have to get in the pool. I encourage you to ask yourself, "If not now, then when?"

Big hairy audacious goals

In our busy consumer and capitalist modern day lives, it's easy to be coaxed into believing bigger is better. Business leaders set 'big hairy audacious goals' (BHAG's) for their organisations. Motivational speakers preach "Aim for the stars, because if you miss at least you'll land on the moon", while talented athletes train for years with their hopes set on Olympic Gold.

We're constantly striving for more: more money, more experiences, more accolades and more attention, while forgetting or just being unaware of how much is really enough. Often we buy into the misbelief that we're less than others based on others having more than we do. Which by the way is a foundational and globally successful strategy used by advertisers to push their products.

A 'caveat emptor' about goals

I drank all the goal setting kool-aid I could drink throughout my narcissistic youth and adult years. However soon after experiencing my 'goal high', I was on the chase for another 'goal high' to replace the last one and with each new goal, came more risk. With the clarity of hindsight I now appreciate this was wrong as it developed into an inner, personally abusive relationship. I never felt good enough, was overly critical of myself, gave myself ultimatums and isolated myself. At the same time my income was skyrocketing and outwardly I was a 'success' however I was stuck on this goal/image treadmill that never let up!

I will save you from the pity party that unfolded, however the experience took me through the most personally challenging, grounding and awakening chapters of my life. Then slowly I began to embrace life again, free from burdens. I began a new journey of experiencing life to its fullest while at the same time renewing my inner peace. Rather than aiming for the stars, I started to mine diamonds and gold in my backyard and I discovered some real beauties!

When is enough, **enough**?

One such diamond came in the form of the business in Cairns. Another came in the form of patience which lead me to a property purchase at 40% of the original price. However by far the most precious discovery was that of 'ENOUGH', as I like to call it. How much is enough is as different to every individual as we are unique, however knowing what it looks like and finding it is transformational.

For me, discovering my 'ENOUGH' has filled the inner void of inadequacy that I had struggled with. I now appreciate and understand that I was overcompensating and masking with BHAG and 'look at me' successes.

Discovering my 'ENOUGH' has also freed me from crippling debt, useless must-haves and superficial relationships. Most importantly, it has allowed me to experience not only financial freedom but a deeper and richer relationship with God, enabling me to receive the spiritual and psychological freedom that comes with this profound and regenerative relationship.

And here's the kicker about discovering 'ENOUGH'. It nurtures oneself to become more genuine and authentic, which is actually an attractive and rare quality in our fast paced, modern world. Simply being ME, is my point of difference.

Moving forward I am motivated to uniquely, 'as God has created me', add more value to others, not because I need them to buy because I already have enough, but because it is the right thing to do, it is my passion and it is God's command.

Final thought: Be kind to yourself. You are important, unique and the winning sperm that won the race of a lifetime!

PETER HORSFIELD

Contributor Profile: Peter is Managing Director of FMW Financial Planning and he has grown the business to become recognised 2007, 2008 and 2010 as National Advisory Practice of the Year. Peter's goal is to help others achieve their goals sooner by delivering both a tailored and effective advice solution built on flexibility and value.

Peter brings with him a wealth of academic and business achievements and experience in creating a unique and best advice business model that put client's interests first.

- Certified Financial Planner (FPA Member) since 2003
- Self Managed Superannuation Fund Specialist (SPAA Member) since 2009
- Diploma Financial Advice (SIA Member) since 1999
- Founder FMW Financial Planning Pty 2005
- Financial Services since 1998
- Trusted Advisor (Values Based Financial Planning) 2010

Self Introduction: Coffee addicted lover of life who lives and breathes epic digital marketing strategies. Living the dream!

Website: www.peterhorsfield.com.au
Facebook: peterhorsfieldcfp
Linkedin: Peter Horsfield
Email: peterhorsfieldcfp@gmail.com

Food for thought

Have you identified an area in your life or business that needs 'massive change'?

Write down the issues. If there is more than one major problem write each one on a different page in your notebook. Now beside the issue, in a different color pen, write down what the situation would look like if it was no longer a problem. This is your goal. Further down the page, write down any steps or solutions you can identify that will move you from the problem to the goal. Add time frames and deadlines. This is your action plan. Who can you share your action plan with? Do you have a mentor or coach who will help you stay on track to see your dreams realised?

Do you need to do further study? If so, what type of study would best suit your needs?

Have you had a scripture, word or sign from God regarding your business? If so, write it down and put it in a prominent place eg. on your fridge or mirror where you will see it every day. If not, ask Him for one.

Have you done any recent assessments to determine where your business is succeeding or failing? Are there any areas that are not productive or generating only low profits? What areas are performing the best? Assessments might be financial reviews, customer feedback surveys or a profit and loss calculation. You don't need to wait until tax time to do accounting reports. Some businesses do them weekly, monthly or quarterly. Decide what you need and work on it.

Peter discovered a number of benefits from simplifying his life and business model. Clarity, peace, health, relationships, confidence, liberation and gratitude. Are you struggling in any of these areas? What can you do to simplify your life so that these areas are addressed and flowing well in your life and business?

What is your self-talk like? Spend a day, writing down all of the things that go through your mind. The things you tell yourself about yourself, your life, your family and your business. This may seem onerous, but it is a worthwhile project. You will be surprised how you can identify thought processes that are either lifting you up or pulling you down. Then you will be in a position to replace negative thoughts with those scriptures, words or signs from God that He has given you.

Chapter Eight
Releasing the Aroma of Christ

It's been a 'God set-me-up' journey all along. The leading of God and relationships developed along the way have built the ministry that I am now a part of. It has been a journey through phases combining ministry and business while being service focused in a community building capacity.

As a pre-teen at about eleven years of age, two profound moments with God were signs of what my business and ministry were to become. The first was when I watched a deaf interpreter in a church and said to God in my heart, "I'll do that for you one day".

Some years later, while sitting in a Bible College class, God recounted that moment, showing me as a vivid memory that has never left me. Toward the end of my second year of Bible College, I felt God say it was time to start a ministry to the deaf community.

Later, in my first year at university, being prophesied over that "[I] am a leader", was so foreign to my mindset. As

I had a vocational desire for the health field, I studied nursing. I have developed a ministry and now a business within the wellness industry and continue to work in nursing.

A new ministry begins

In 1999, I commenced a Certification in Australian Sign Language and pastored a local deaf community group of Auslan users. In 2000, I became a licensed minister and registered the business name 'Signs Ministries'. I had the best mentors for the first years of pastoring who were able to direct me to ordination in a faith based licensing organisation. As a ministry to the deaf, we are effective in outreaches throughout Queensland and team with local ministries in overseas countries to minister to deaf adults and children. My strengths in ministry are pastoral care and teaching.

The 'Signs Ministries' vision grew global in 2008 with a plan for the Gospel to be accessed by deaf communities of all nations in their native sign language. Signs Ministries Pty Ltd was registered as a charitable trust and the move toward global reach had begun.

By 2010, as I completed interpreter qualifications, a business arm of the ministry was growing. Auslan Christian Interpreters Network began a few years earlier, for supporting interpreters in the Christian sector, while organising payment for the work of the interpreters at Christian events. This part of the ministry felt easier, sensing God's grace on it for the mission of honouring the work of interpreters as an integral part of the ministry team.

In 2016 the first planning steps for creating an online Auslan Bible College for the Australian deaf community were put in place.

My gifts developed with the roles of administration, as the Auslan Christian Interpreters Network required coordination as an agency. We have experienced God's blessing on the business with increasing numbers of interpreters being available to fulfil every assignment we have been tasked with while organising the rostering and honorarium payments to the interpreters. The business arm grew through relationships with major Christian organisations and later with the addition of secular organisations and small businesses.

Experiencing the aroma of Jesus

The second profound moment has always stayed hidden as a personal worship moment but it was in preparation for the business opportunity I currently work in. As an eleven year old, I experienced the aroma of the presence of Jesus.

Later at sixteen, a prophesy about leading worship and aroma was spoken over my life. I questioned it for many years, because the 'worship leading' I knew of church was not for me. I don't sing and I don't play instruments. Later, through the deaf ministry, I realised that deaf people worshiped differently so I learned to worship in a sensory and more visual way. Interpreting worship in sign language is different again.

Aromatically, I didn't understand this aspect of worship until I was introduced to pure essential oils in 2013. The first contact I had with essential oils was through deaf community relationships. Deaf friends were sharing the opportunity for natural plant therapeutics at a time I was seeking to start a home based business.

Aromatic oils in the Bible

I studied aroma in the Bible and I discovered that there are many links between aroma and worship. God has enhanced in my memory that first instance of the aroma of Jesus' presence and a friend with me at the time also remembered it. I recreated that aroma using essential oils as described in the Bible and it was the same fragrance we experienced as eleven year olds in 1984, which my friend positively confirmed in 2016!

When I reflect on Romans 12:1–2, I find each person's reasonable worship is the presentation of our total being in service to God. It's an ongoing development. The processes of living for God and being renewed in mind by His Word has physical implications. The tools we use to sustain the process need to be God-honouring for mind and body, and this is why I align to using essential oils as much as fruit and vegetables as God's design for us.

'Essential Grace' became the registered business through which I express my passion and find many opportunities for teaching health and wellbeing using essential oils. I have found a business niche that I can teach from a Biblical perspective and within the framework of teaching Christian lifestyle principles which I find very fulfilling. I am certified in a massage modality using the essential oils, which in itself lends to personal ministry and I create homemade essential oil products for sale.

The 'Essential Grace' business supports a Thai ministry in the process of selling bracelets made of beads for diffuser jewellery. This Thai ministry relationship developed also from 'Signs Ministries' activity through a partnership supporting the vision for developing an online Auslan Bible College. A founder of the Thai ministry is deaf, working as the Dean of Studies of an international Bible College.

Through the essential oils business, I am a mentor to other emerging leaders who are building their own businesses. There is much personal development in that journey, which is mutually supportive in networking, a process I find comes easily as it is another strength of mine. Not dissimilar to Christian ministry, a vision develops out of fulfilling some values attached to a purpose for doing the business. Firstly comes the personal vision and then the leap to a larger, possibly even global vision. Any person's vocation or business can have global reach but their passion must sustain them through the activities or phases of the vision being fulfilled.

'Essential Grace' is a growing business and the increasing profit is providing the funding for the global vision of 'Signs Ministries'. I am doing all that I love, serving people's health and wellbeing with naturally created resources and serving the God-given vision for a global ministry to the deaf. Together, both are the vehicles of what God has purposed in my life and they are developing me into the entrepreneur I need to be to bring it all to pass.

God given desires of the heart have purpose!

I have spent many weekends in church and additional Christian conferences and I have heard a lot through my lifetime. Things to avoid, things that are offensive to God. Sometimes it's said in context of theology, sometimes it is man's opinion. A phrase that stuck in my memory from a preacher was "aromatherapy is witchcraft". That memory dates back to sometime in the 1980's, to be wary of aromatherapy plus everything else that went with it. However, I will not use such things as crystals and astrology even though they are often associated with aromatherapy from a marketing viewpoint. The problem is that a blanket statement can warp a true definition of something natural because of the way it can be misused.

I've come to an experiential and Biblical knowledge that God likes aroma (See Exodus chapter 31) and we are the aroma of life as followers of Jesus. (See 2 Corinthians chapter 2). Experientially, I've smelt the aroma of the presence of Jesus, and others have experienced this, too. The message from the preacher in the 80's, should have been 'aromatherapy is a tool', that could be used for either good or evil. Anything is a tool, and it depends on whether the user has a positive or negative intention in employing that tool that will determine its use for good or evil. Believers have control over what they judge as right or wrong and a responsibility to align their perspective with Biblical representation.

My business is largely informing people about what essential oils are and how to use them. By design, they are compatible with human biology for health and emotional wellbeing, supportive to every tissue and cell type. I've offered essential oils, which are aromatic compounds, to Christians of various backgrounds. One has recounted the above 'demonic' influence associated with using essential oils, because a 'Pastor said it'. Another reaction I've received when presenting essential oils for health to Christians is, "I believe in healing and I stand on God's promises." I'm sure God would be just as impressed with that person for eating their vegetables!

Our health is important
We are responsible for what we know to do with our health and the Bible rates health right near the top of mankind's

priorities! Essential oil use is still gaining popularity and attention. The market has always been flooded with natural health promoting juices, supplements, foods, etc. and we have a choice to accept anything offered to us for our health and wellbeing but we also have a responsibility to do our research so we know if the product we want to use will do what it says it will and be what we need.

Using what God intended for our good is wisdom. I encourage any person to do what their conscience is leading them to do. Preventative care for the body and its systems is personal and a social responsibility.

In giving information I do emphasise the empowerment in having the resources to support ourselves. I share my experience and allow others to be able to hold the same vision for their own health. I share mine as follows: "A few years ago, when I found essential oils, I knew they were an integral part of the combination for all things, I believed, that created wellbeing. Integrating the oils into my family's daily lives was a major step in completing the picture of health. The oils are now the foundation of a sustainable, preventative and responsive health care model in our home."

As a vision grows, so does the number of lives that can and will be touched.

Phases or leaps could describe the way the ministry journey has progressed from local to global vision. The lengths of each phase may be characterised by the development of ministry activities or business related activities but always running an x y axis of relationship to God and the terms of the many relationships that supported and partnered with 'Signs Ministries' with each leap.

God creates, through a humble person, a vision that meets a niche in life that may look to only appeal to a small percentage of people. As the vision grows, so does the number of lives that can and will be touched. It's important to have a global vision just as God's mission is global. Initially, a small business vision serves your family and your local area. Your larger vision usually incorporates all the leadership and processes to take you on your entrepreneurial journey so you can serve internationally. A strong global vision will carry you through all the experiences of business and ministry.

- God given desires of the heart have purpose. That purpose creates meaning in your life and fulfils your creativity in business.

- Businesses grow by relationships. The more aligned that relationship is to the Kingdom of God the more relevant the business is to those it serves.

CHARMAYNE CHINNERY

Contributor Profile: Charmayne is the CEO at Essential Grace, a business specialising in the use of essential oils for better health and well being. She is passionate about helping people renew mindsets and wellbeing so they can be the best version of themselves.

Self Introduction: Passionate, empowered and making an impact.

Facebook: essentialgrace1

Email: charmayne.essentialgrace@gmail.com

Food for thought

Have you had a 'profound moment' where God has spoken to your heart or you have been moved in a way that has impacted your life and vision? Have you written it down and/or shared it with others?

How does this 'profound moment' affect your life, ministry or business today?

How can you use your business to mentor other people or minister into the lives of others less fortunate?

Is your business a vehicle to seeing God's plans and purposes realised in your life? How is this happening?

Have you had someone speak negatively about your business? How have you overcome this negativity? Are you still trying to overcome it? If so, who can help you?

How do you describe yourself and your business? Write this down in a few short sentences and memorise it. This is particularly helpful when you meet new people and they ask about you or about your business and it is essential if you attend any networking events.

How would you class your business: local, national or international? Could or should this change? What influence do you want your business to have?

Chapter Nine

Learning from Our Mistakes

I've been in business for over thirty years. My journey began when I started doing a milk run at just thirteen years of age. At sixteen I was managing the milk run. My journey then led me to mechanics. It was while I was there that I met my lovely wife and in 1984 we were married.

1985 saw me then move into an engineering and mechanical business in Littlehampton, South Australia. A few years later, we started a self-storage business, the business I still manage and grow today. We started from scratch with little experience and even less finance. Not being an academic student or qualified in tertiary schooling has probably helped in being adventurous and thinking outside of the square. My school report used to say, 'David would do better if he attended class'.

Running your own business is great but it can also be full of highs and lows. An entrepreneur often sees something before it is created or creates something better than what has already been produced previously. Opportunity is seen as possibility. Entrepreneurship is the art of seeing something before it is a reality.

When we started our self storage business we went to the State Bank and borrowed $6,000 then walked up to the Commonwealth Bank and used that as a deposit for a $32,000 loan to buy our first storage block in 1987. I could see the vision for my business, I believed I could build it and I had the tenacity and some experience to be able to make my dream a reality.

This industry was in its infancy then and we had to evolve by trying ideas, some good and some not so good, but we chose new paths, took action when it was needed and learnt from the outcomes.

Fear can rob us of our potential because we don't want to fail!

Something isn't necessarily wrong just because it didn't work in a particular instance. This is a cultural misconception. We are conditioned to believe that if something hasn't been successful then it is wrong. Sometimes our best lessons come out of our mistakes and if we hadn't 'failed' we wouldn't have seen the opportunity that was a winner or taken different steps to get us there. Our business success has been an evolution of identifying what customers were asking for, researching the possibilities, doing our due diligence and where feasible, putting ideas and proposals into action.

Fear can often rob us of our potential because we don't want to fail. We think that if we don't act we can't fail but an entrepreneurial spirit overcomes fear and sees the end product or result and aims for that.

Thirty years later we have six storage facilities and a large number of properties.

Don't conform to the ways of the world but trade with integrity, honesty and a servant heart!

Running our own business as Christians has given us freedom and confidence to stand firm in the business model we have. This doesn't mean that we have not had our ups and downs. It has not always been smooth sailing.

There have been times when we have pushed too hard and ended up creating difficulties for ourselves. Being a Christian doesn't exempt or discount you from tough times. But it is in these times that you can just stand firm, learn and move on. We can't conform to the ways of the world. We must choose to trade and run our businesses with integrity, honesty and a servant heart.

When I was in my twenties, I made a decision that no matter what circumstances were before me I would choose to remain who I believe I am, who God has called me to be. I decided that I would be in church every Sunday. Church isn't about a religion, it is about meeting with people who have a common belief and being challenged and accountable. Having fellowship regularly is essential for personal growth and mental stability.

I have made the decision to stay generous. Helping others has always been important to me so for eight years I served on the board of the Australasian Self Storage Association helping people starting storage businesses and sharing our experience with others. I have been blessed to be able to take my experience and knowledge to new levels in consulting and helping others who are starting out.

Now is the time when we decide to change our future!

It was only a few years ago that we went through an extremely tight and difficult period. We were close to losing everything and I was given the opportunity to help a Sydney group build two houses in a village in Fiji. This became a pivotal point in realising what we have and how we can help those in less fortunate parts of the world in some small way.

Sharing time with these Fijian people and seeing how little they have, yet they are so happy and entrepreneurial, has impacted me greatly. Since then I have completed seven builds and going to Fiji has become time out for me to serve and to reset my compass.

Our time on earth is small in the grand scheme of things so I earnestly believe that we must seize opportunity when it presents itself. How many times do you hear "I wish I had bought back then when it was so cheap". Hindsight is a great teacher but being an entrepreneur means having foresight and vision and you soon learn that there is no better time than now.

Now is the time when we decide to change our future. There is no value in looking back on what we could have done. Decisions are made at the time based on what we know at that time. It is all just part of the journey.

There will always be challenges and I've pushed through

many in my time in business. Financial issues would have to be some of the hardest. There are many things out of our control, like how banks treat you when rules change, retrospective laws are enacted and economies shift.

You have three options in difficult times. You can blame God, you can try and deal with it the best way you can in your own strength or you can turn to God and seek His wisdom and guidance.

Think about it! From what you know of God, do you really think He is out to take you down? No. Circumstances change and problems arise all the time but there is one thing I know for sure, it's impossible to get through without divine intervention.

An important strategy is to let other people speak into your world. A mentor is essential to give perspective, counsel and support. I was privileged to have a friend, Eric Paschke, who was a great influence, advisor and listener for my formative journey. We used to chat in his backyard next to the fruit tree that was grafted to bear two fruits. He left so much wisdom to so many people – he is missed.

Knowing that your trust in God is greater than what you face, is so important!

The devil will try to distract you with fear along the way. But fear is only 'false evidence appearing real'. It's an attempt to distract you from trusting God, finding a solution and moving forward. We can only be concerned about what we can change, the rest is best left with God. Worrying about what we can't change only bogs us down in anxiety and 'what-if's'. It's an unrealistic Christian expectation that we can fix everything and be all things to all people.

> *For no temptation (no trial regarded as enticing to sin), [no matter how it comes or where it leads] has overtaken you and laid hold on you that is not common to man [that is, no temptation or trial has come to you that is beyond human resistance and that is not adjusted and adapted and belonging to human experience, and such as man can bear]. But God is faithful [to His Word and to His compassionate nature], and He [can be trusted] not to let you be tempted and tried and assayed beyond your ability and strength of resistance and power to endure, but with the temptation He will [always] also provide the way out (the means of escape to a landing place), that you may be capable and strong and powerful to bear up under it patiently.*
>
> ### 1 Corinthians 10:13

God will never take us through more than we can deal with. If we abide in him and He abides in us, then nothing can happen that will surpass your ability and capacity. Even though we experience trying days with highs, lows and plateaus, we can remain stable knowing that God is walking with us.

When my capacity is challenged, growth happens!

I'm always looking to grow, stagnation isn't an option for me. I'm not scared of change, in fact I welcome it. It's quite often during the times when I am experiencing the lows, that I grow the most. It doesn't matter what comes my way, God has it. In fact, it's been in the midst of some of the hardest times that fresh ideas have come to me. These ideas just feel like they are God inspired. There is a strong point of difference and they renew excitement and expectation within me.

> *'If ye abide in me, and my words abide in you, ye shall ask what ye will, and it shall be done unto you.'*
> **John 15:7 (KJV)**

Our business is constantly evolving. There are always new opportunities for a business to grow. We have had to embrace new technologies to make sure we are presented in the best possible way. Google 360 recently came through one of our storage sites to create a video for us so people don't even have to visit us to see what our facility looks like.

Innovative marketing is a must in business so don't be afraid to explore avenues and different opportunities but always monitor the results. If it doesn't work, it doesn't work. Scrap it.

Twenty years ago, we started a remote self storage facility

in Victor Harbor, South Australia, built as if it was next door to our office at Mt Barker, using technology to run it and it was unheard of back then. We took a risk with minimal cash flow and it paid off. While extra cash would have been great at these growth times, I have had to get back to basics and do some of the groundwork myself a lot of the time. It's only been a few years since I stopped digging holes. Sometimes you just have to put the hard yards in. Now I spend more time overseeing these tasks.

I can see a few more storage facilities in Adelaide in the future and I can also see growth and influence in other ways, too. It is so important to embrace what's happening in your industry, to listen to what people are saying and then share that knowledge, understanding and experience with others. I have business mates in the same industry across the world now! In fact, I even catch up with some of my competitors here for the odd meal.

Have a business plan. Write down what you want to achieve, how you want to achieve it and where you want to get to. Condense this to one page and look at it monthly. Don't write a business plan of 40 pages explaining how many impossible things you want to achieve. Keep it Basic, Simple and Achievable. Let it evolve. Don't intend it to be rigid. Adapt it every month so as circumstances change, industry evolves and opportunities arise, you can align your structure with change. Keep it simple. This doesn't mean you can't have a lot of things happening or trying innovative ideas but be clear yourself about what you want to achieve. Make it viable. Think reality in your circumstances. Don't intend on spending a million dollars in the first year. Be realistic and achievable.

Some of your best seasons will be out the other side of difficulty!

When I look back on my journey, I can see that it really helps to have certain traits that can help a person be successful. You must have passion, you need to be really invested in what you do. This will help you push through the hard times. It's also important to have stickability and perseverance. We can't run when things get tough. Some of your best seasons will be out the other side of difficulty.

As a Christian in business I think it's important to have a servant heart. People really know the difference between someone just pushing their agenda and someone who genuinely wants to serve. It's one of the traits that make us different as Christian business owners. Following on from that, is the importance of putting yourself in your customer's shoes. I ask myself questions like: What do I expect from a service provider? Would I expect good customer service or someone that's argumentative? What would make me want to come back to this business? I can then structure my business model to make sure that my customers' experience is a positive one.

The culture that I build my business on is one of fairness, honesty and integrity. These things matter to God, to me and to my customers. I can drive a hard deal in business but I never take advantage of the customer. My deals are competitive but fair. You need to be able to buy at the right price and sell at the right price and have a margin that makes you money.

Money increases your ability to influence others!

As a Christian entrepreneur, you want to make a difference in people's lives. You want them to know you are different, you want them to ask why you are different. Being a Christian in business is more about who you are rather than just telling people what they need. Relationships are the vital key in our influence with others. Customers see the difference in how we relate to them. It's the approachable interaction and the way they feel accepted when they are around us. It is positive impact without the Bible bashing. It's what makes Christian entrepreneurs stand out.

I've never had an issue with money. Money, when made in an ethical way, increases your ability to influence others. I can still remember that first time I went to Fiji with the team. Our business was not going well, times were really tough and we were about to lose everything. But I made that sacrifice financially to go, to invest in something greater than my situation and it was a truly life changing experience. Money allows you to do things for others that you wouldn't have been able to do otherwise. Not only have I been able to help people in Fiji but I am also building a legacy for my kids and their kids for long after I'm gone.

As a Christian entrepreneur, the question always needs to be: How can I make this work? What do I need to push through, to achieve that shift and new growth out the other side? Where is my complete trust, in the economy or in God? When we get used to challenging what is, with the view of creating the new, with God on our side we cannot fail. Don't be afraid to have Christian friends around you, to support you, to encourage you and to back you in prayer. God never wanted us to live this life on our own and it is the same in business.

In summary: Dream big. Persist through tough times. Find a mentor. Have a simple one page agenda. Get involved with something outside your world. Be regularly and actively involved in a church and ENJOY LIFE.

DAVID DADDOW

Contributor Profile: David has been involved in the self storage industry for thirty years, seeing the highs and lows of business expansion to now include multiple locations. He is an industry leader, serving on an Australasian Board. David also project manages house builds in Fiji with C3 Church.

Self Introduction: An entrepreneur at heart, he's a quiet but highly respected achiever, and loves living in the Adelaide Hills.

Website: https://ableselfstorage.com.au/

Facebook: david.daddow.1

Linkedin: David Daddow

Email: selfstoragesa@gmail.com

SSOA Board member: www.selfstorage.org.au/about/board-of-directors

Food for thought

What is your vision for your business? Have you written it down? If not, do so.

Fear of failure can rob us of potential, progress and learning opportunities. Are there any areas where you have not moved forward because of a fear of failure? Identify what the worst is that can happen, then work towards your goal. If you do fail, look for the lessons that you need to learn so you can try again. Sometimes God uses failure in one area to turn us to another option or opportunity. Failure is never final unless you make it so.

Is your business identified by integrity, honesty and service? If not, do you need to integrate these qualities into your business?

Have you thought about and written down your goals for a year from now, five years' time and ten years' time? What processes or procedures will need to be put in place to achieve these goals? Can you identify any areas that will need to be addressed?

If you are experiencing difficult times right now, are you blaming God or trying to do things in your own strength? Have you spent time with God seeking His wisdom and guidance?

Are you fearful of change? Are you willing to learn new things, try new things and grow in your ability and capacity? These are essential traits for business owners because businesses are organic by nature. The world is constantly changing, advertising methods change, people's needs and expectations change and business practices change. We must be willing to change if and when required.

Have you ever done a 'secret shopper' or 'undercover boss' exercise with your business? How do you know what your customer's needs are? Is your staff acting in you and your business's best interests? How can your business model reflect good customer service, develop rapport with your customers and ensure that customers not only return, but that they bring others with them?

What is your point of difference in your business? How do you impart your point of difference to your staff and present it to your customers or clients?

How do you view money? How do you use money? Are you selfish or generous? Do you see money as a way to help and influence others or are you chasing a big bank account?

Chapter Ten
Nothing is Wasted

I was blessed to grow up in church as a kid in a small country town called Emerald in Central Queensland. My family weren't just church goers though, my parents served for many years wherever needed and it was only natural in a small country church that as myself and my brothers grew older that we too, began to serve in varying capacities. It wasn't something we had to consider, it was just a natural progression. When I graduated from Sunday school, I moved into serving and helping out there. Thinking back, even at the young age of twelve, I loved working with our leaders, planning what we were going to do and the challenge of how to see those plans implemented.

Youth group was the next natural step and when I was old enough to become a leader, I stepped up, carrying various responsibilities. I really hated high school because I was bullied. I begged my parents to let me homeschool grades eleven and twelve. Apart from not liking high school, we were wasting a lot of time on library, lunch and sport (ouch!). I knew I could get my schooling done quicker and more efficiently leaving me room to do other things that interested me more than basketball. A pretty big call as a fourteen year old. I guess I was always doing things outside the box, I didn't want to just be doing things the way everyone else was doing stuff, I had things to do, places to be. I was invested in something bigger than myself and I had other priorities (rightly or wrongly as a teenager). I loved just being left to learn at my own pace, on my own terms, to get it done quicker, which funnily enough is the basis of how I run my marketing company. It's amazing how the skills you learn as a child and teenager can really form the basis of your future success. Nothing is wasted.

Juggling homeschooling and some casual work, I became available to help my youth pastor roll out Teen Challenge programs at our church amongst other things. Being on hand, being available to step in when needed, finding solutions, generating ideas, and contributing to the impact we were having on the local kids, was just me. It was what I was created for. We were encouraged as youth leaders to be prepared to run with anything, at anytime. Such an amazing skill to have and something I have continued to build into my business. It means I can MC an event at twenty four hours notice (yes that really did happen), rise to any challenge set before me and actively find solutions for problems. This one skill alone has helped me stand out from my competitors.

Music was a huge part of my life with my entire family being musically gifted and my dad being music director at our church for a number of 'Maranatha' years (remember those?). Music and worship was the foundation of our existence (though as a child I didn't quite realise this at the time). I'd grown up worshipping from a very young age and these days, worship still plays such an important part of my life. After all, we wouldn't be here if it wasn't for our amazing God, breathing life and sustaining us daily.

I started playing keyboard in church at twelve, worship leading at sixteen, worship leading from the keys at seventeen. I was an active member of the church worship team for many years. I lived and breathed music, I still do. We were the largest church in our region, we were the Regional Youth Alive hosts and we all had so many fun times together. I loved being resourceful, finding solutions and being part of a team. More passions I now live out in my business. Fourteen years later, I was to pick up that keyboard and sing in a music team again, with no skill lost.

> I loved those early years of being engaged in ministry, and while I had some idea that God had a unique plan for my life, never in a million years did I ever see my future being what it is today.

I was married at twenty one, and left 'home' and all of the things that I was involved in, to move to Adelaide to attend Bible college with my then husband. I was scared that I would never be on a music team ever again or be a leader in any capacity. I had a sense that God had a purpose for my life and while I had a clear picture in my head of how that purpose would play out, I was very, very wrong! I loved my three and a half years at Bible College. Ok, maybe not the assignments and exams but the community and eye opening lectures were so amazing. The time with other Christians to focus on good quality discussions and learning about leadership and pastoral roles was such a highlight. I loved the ministry hours we had to do. It gave me new contacts and a huge range of experiences from preaching, to planning programs, to directing kids camps. It was just me, authentically aligned with what God had put within me.

The intentional time and interaction with other students as representatives of other denominations was so enriching and broadened my view of God, Christianity and life. I was the only Pentecostal at that Bible college and out of my three years there, I was Student President for two. You see, it was becoming clear that everywhere I went I naturally ended up in leadership positions. This time at Bible college was no different. But, due to circumstances out of my control, I had to give up many great opportunities to serve in local churches in pastoral roles. I was broken, my heart was torn out. All I ever wanted, was to be in ministry, to serve, and I had to give that all away. I was sold out for the cause. This wasn't how it was meant to be! I thought my life was over, that my best years were done. I was in a different state away from all of my family, feeling the brunt of difficult seasons and sick as a dog. I had no direction, no vision and was coming to terms with just being a stay at home mum, which in itself is not a bad thing, but the frustration of knowing I was made for more and the inability to see that come to fruition, was real. After Bible college, we found it hard at the time to find a new home church. Nothing really seemed to fit. Not being planted in any one particular church for fourteen years has been tough.

Tough seasons build depth of character, understanding, a brighter fire, and a stronger foundation.

It's amazing, that as I look back over the last fourteen years, I can see that God was always there, protecting me (though it didn't feel like it at the time), keeping me on track and guiding me in the smallest of ways. He didn't give up on me or throw my destiny and to-do-list out the window. He was just waiting for the right time and his timing is always perfect. My journey did not pan out the way I thought it would, but God never gave up on me. Sometimes we are forced to surrender the outcome to God. It's tough when you really have nothing left, no direction and no motivation but God really came through for me in the end, fourteen years later. Now I've come to realise that we need to surrender up, not only the outcomes, the things we think God wants us to do and the situations we need shifted but we also need to surrender the whole process. His ways are higher than our ways and his plans for us are bigger than we can imagine. The opportunities he has put before me, have really blown my mind. While I felt the best was over, his plans for my life were just starting to unfold.

Don't base your future on what is directly in and around you now. Lift your focus to God and let him unfold his plans and purposes for your life in ways you could never have imagined.

I stand in awe at how God has not wasted one single situation, one single tough season, one single win. I would not be the person I am today, in the positions I hold today, doing the things I am doing today, if I hadn't experienced those difficult times. I am a completely different person with a certain depth of character, a better understanding of how tough things get for people around us, deeper strength and resilience and a better understanding of how important it is for us to shine our light by living an authentic existence.

Was I disappointed that my life did not head towards full-time ministry in 2003? Absolutely! But once my expectation and picture of how it should have been was put aside, I just got on with what I could do at the time (which was starting a home-based business from scratch), utilising what was in front of me. Over time things started shifting. On a practical level, I knew what my passions were so I started to incorporate those into my decisions. The rest is history.

> **Action is crucial to moving out of tough situations, even if you are unsure which direction you should be moving in. If the least you can do is reposition yourself for change, then so be it. Action shifts things.**

God still moved me towards his plans and purposes for my life throughout those times when I thought he wasn't there but he did it in the most creative way, utilising every part of who I am and what I do, to live an authentic life. Now I feel completely where I need to be, doing what I need to be doing. It's a path I could never have ever dreamed I would be on. I'm in ministry twenty-four hours a day, seven days a week. I don't stop work to 'do' ministry and have an impact. I am on the ground day in, day out and God uses me in the most random of ways. I serve (carry out ministry) in the smallest of ways, to the biggest, the majority of it between Monday and Saturday. My life, my journey through the highs and lows, my testimony of God's goodness and sovereignty in my life, his provision, his protection, his positioning me, all contribute to the message and impact that God wants me to have on those around me. Our greatest message is our lives, not the words we speak.

I must have been bored, or God was at work

My twins boys were just nine months old when I decided to start my business. I had been playing around with some smaller hobby businesses, which ended up becoming a tax writeoff for the following three years (nothing is wasted!), not financially profitable at all. But I did dip my toe in business and I learned so much through those small steps while I was finding my way. While I enjoyed doing the crafty stuff at the time, the financial gain wasn't really worth it for the time and effort I was putting in. I created a Facebook presence for one of my hobby businesses and realised that Facebook really was a great tool in growing brand awareness. In 2010, businesses were really only starting to utilise Facebook. I could see that we could be using it better, that there was more potential in what we could do with this platform and I lived and breathed Facebook to learn how to use it. I managed to inherit an amazing business brain from my mother and I was starting to see how I could make some extra money helping brands online with creative but affordable solutions.

I started creating welcome pages (yes, back in those days) and then started to add new services over time as I had different ideas or saw a need. I was in my creative element and also making some money. To build the number of people on my page I decided to start doing some free webinars. I ran 'The Ins and Outs of Facebook' webinar about fifteen times across a two to three year period, with the biggest webinar hosting 94 people. I always had new clients in my inbox the following morning and educating people via webinars, workshops and e-courses has continued to be my #1 lead generation tool. By the end of a workshop, people would know whether they could connect with me, whether they needed my skillset or whether they needed my motivation and creativity to help them grow their businesses. I also got quite a few referrals over the years. As my skills grew and opportunities arose, my business grew.

I remember starting out at $25 per hour, happy to just be working from home around the kids. I made a decision early on, to choose excellence over perfection. I didn't have all the answers, no-one does really. I just wanted to give my best with what I had at the time. It can be daunting to look at how easy it seems for everyone else in business, but we are all on the same journey (and let's not base judgement on what we see on social media! That's not always the full story). Perfection is one of the things that holds us back the most in life. The truth is, what perfection is to one person, is different for the next. Perfection stops us from putting our hand up to help, stifles action in business and at work and stops us from achieving our full potential.

> **Choose excellence over perfection the outcome will always be your best.**

My first year was a tough one. I ended up in hospital in June of that year (my third month in business) with Pneumonia, Sarcoidosis relapse and another infection. It took twelve months to recover, but I pushed through. I can remember putting the twins to bed at 7:00pm, going to bed for forty minutes to regain some strength, before getting up to be online and vibrant for an hour at 8:00pm. Hectic times, but it was so worth it. We experience many ups and downs in business, but if we take the situations around us as a sign that we are on the wrong track all the time, we'd never get anywhere, we would never start anything and we would keep stopping short of our potential. I'm so glad I kept moving forward, even if at times it was one step forward, two steps back. You need to push through to see your passion become a reality. In my eight years of business, there have been seasons where I've only had the strength to shuffle emails, while other days, I'm on a world domination mission. I can be anywhere in between at other times. Stay true to what you believe you are meant to be doing, know what authentically aligns with who you are, ride out the tough times, celebrate the good times. We've got this.

Business success: 75% the person behind it

I am a big believer that the success of a business is 75% the person behind it. I don't say that because I am anything special. I never would have labelled myself overly smart, but I did make some choices (without initially realising it), that I would live a life of learning; that I would embrace and allow my business to evolve; that I would be fiercely committed and driven, but flexible and embracing; that I would cultivate fresh ideas and creativity, and all of these things have contributed to my success to this day. This has been crucial for me as I never attended university. I am completely self-taught. Yes, completely, self-taught. A degree is not always necessarily required for you to start a business and be successful (of course, if you want to be a doctor or a lawyer it is crucial.) Maybe another qualification would be enough for your needs. Just know that there are alternative and sometimes smarter ways to achieve things and set yourself up. Do your research and take action.

> **When starting a business, we need to make many choices. Those choices begin with us having the courage to make them.**

Success is about intentionally cultivating, intentionally focusing, intentionally learning, intentionally positioning yourself for more. It is defined by the makeup of your beliefs and mindsets, and the action that you first, then your team, take. It's about what fuels you as a person, the things you are passionate about, the things that light you up, that connect in with who you are. There are a variety of reasons why we want to 'challenge what is, and create something new'. The good and the bad become driving factors in our success. Business success starts with us and how we turn things around for the good. You are the person that drives your team, motivates them, acknowledges them and challenges them to greater learning and better results which in turn, facilitates growth.

You see it's one thing to have a marketing degree, it's another thing to be constantly on the cutting edge, reliable, creative, driven and cultivating a 'can do' attitude. In the absence of a degree, these qualities that I have worked to build into my life and business have made me more money in the long run. It's hard to believe I've hit a six figure income, without a degree. Having a contractor on your team that can just roll with what's needed at the drop of a hat, is very attractive for small to medium businesses as well as corporate clients, especially if they don't want to be necessarily employing more staff. Rather than having a one size fits all approach, we spend time working out what their current situation is and what their vision and goals are for the future. We vision build where we think they could go and present options and possibilities that suit their business style, financial commitment and staffing options. Having a 'one size fits all' solution is very dangerous and highly impractical. People want your guidance, but they also love to work with people with a can-do attitude. People that go and find out the answers they need, that are happy to learn when they come across something they don't know how to do yet.

As entrepreneurs, the best thing we can do in life and business is challenge what is and create something new. A new norm, a new service, a new sphere of influence, a smarter way to do things. It's time to take things to new levels.

We have a profound opportunity to contribute to the world around us and make it a better place.

I drove myself nuts with hundreds of business ideas, things I could do, courses I could write, proposals I could develop. I pushed through until I found something that authentically aligned me with my passions and purpose on this earth. Then, like many other entrepreneurs, I had to be confident in my choice to start a marketing company and hold off on the other ideas for a while. As entrepreneurs, we will always be blessed with the ability to generate new ideas, but there is also a time when we need to focus and build on the task we have committed to. I do enjoy working on one development project at any given time, along with what I am doing with Market Me Marketing. This just keeps me on the cutting edge, always building something new. If you find yourself coming up with lots of ideas, get them down on paper and do a little research on their viability then choose one to work on until complete.

Learn then earn

As a digital marketer, it is crucial that I stay up to date with the changes in my industry. Algorithms can shift within hours, Google can change how they rate websites, Facebook can roll out major changes to logo shapes, all within a matter of minutes. People expect that we stay up to date with what's happening in our industry. But I want to take this one step further into intentional learning (which just becomes the way you roll). When I started out, I disliked technology. My mum bought my first domain name for me as I was scared I was going to break the internet. I only had very basic skills. A few years later, clients started asking for Wordpress help. I hated Wordpress, mainly because I didn't understand it. I chose to push through the, 'I have no idea what I'm doing', and the frustrations associated with diving in the deep end, to today being able to build Wordpress websites, manage them and troubleshoot problems. Solving problems still plagues me regularly, but I always choose to learn and push through until it's fixed! Today, Wordpress website work is at least 50% of what I do. I would have been missing out on all that work and being able to provide my clients with a complete service, if I hadn't chosen to learn.

> **The more you learn the more you earn!**

In the early days, I remember doing a ten minute social media slot '#thatsacrime' at a business networking event. In the room listening to me speak, was a couple from an Adelaide based RTO (Registered Training Organisation). They came up to me and asked if I would be interested in a one hour 'guest speaker' slot in some of their business courses. One of my passions was educating and empowering people, but I hadn't had a chance to fulfil that role to his point. Of course, I said yes!

> **It's amazing how when you know what lights you up, what your passions are, what you are destined to do, saying yes and no becomes a lot easier. It either aligns or it doesn't. Over time you become more confident making and standing by your decisions.**

I was also asked to manage their social media profiles and help with basic web edits, work I continue to do even to this day. A few years later, they asked if I wanted to pursue training a bit more, by doing the Certificate IV Training and Assessment so I could train whole days. I jumped at the opportunity, knowing this was something completely aligned with who I was and what I believed I was called to do. I then went on to train staff for whole days ($600+ a day), instead of my one hour guest speaker time slots.

I've since gone on to write my own workshops, webinars and courses, and I am regularly asked to run workshops on behalf of Councils and other business and social networks and at local business events. Training and empowering, two of my passions, go hand in hand so well with marketing. Your passions, most likely go hand in hand with what you find yourself doing today. If you feel frustrated and a bit out of order or there are things you haven't ticked off yet, it's a great time to ask yourself how you can upskill in those areas and grow that bottom line. It might be that you still work for someone else but feel frustrated. Can you change industries or get a different job that aligns more with your passions? It's definitely easier and more fulfilling to do something you love, that connects in with who you are. There is a certain flow that can't be fully experienced any other way.

There is always a creative solution to every challenge.

It's just about making that decision to live life on the edge and seek out what it is you need to find. My work doesn't feel like work because I'm living out each of my passions. And that shows in how I run my business and how I make people in my sphere of influence feel. I love what I do and it shows. Not only that, it's infectious. People can't help but notice you. It's not hard to stand out these days. I'm confident that I am doing the right thing for work, in running my business and while the model may change over time, I'll be confident knowing what I know, to make those bigger decisions in the future.

Decide to be intentional about cultivating an atmosphere of learning. The sky's the limit. The world really is your oyster. It's amazing how, when you learn more, you have the capacity to earn more. Your confidence grows and so does your client's confidence in you. You can upsell to your clients and offer a complete solution and confidently charge more for your services.

My question to you is, what can you learn that will enable you to grow your bottom line? Is there something that you could add to your current offering that will help your clients and thereby grow your business?

Life, Business, Service and Ministry
Life, business, service and ministry are all intertwined. People don't understand why I don't take four weeks off a year, why I struggle to stop on Saturdays and even some Sundays. The best answer I can give is that everything is so authentically aligned, it's a natural progression. It is an existence that is not contradictory in any way. Let's face it, a big part of the reason we want to start a business, is so that we can work hours that suit and do more of what lights us up. It makes complete sense. Instead of taking holidays, I do the things I want to do during the week. I might take my kids away for a week here and there and just do the minimum or sneak in a few things when it's quiet. I go and get my nails done, enjoy a massage, lunch with my friends and weekends away for work. I'll trek my three kids to Queensland for a few weeks and just work remotely and nothing changes business wise. The simple things that I enjoy, that are hard to do when you are working forty hours a week or more in an office for someone else, keep me balanced. Most people can only dream of having the capacity to do what you want when you want. It's an existence worth fighting for.

> "Success is doing what you want to do, when you want, where you want, with whom you want, as much as you

want."
Tony Robbins

It's success on your own terms, your best life. It's loving what you do and how you do it. The hard part is that most people don't understand or get it. I've copped quite a lot of flack over the years from those that don't understand why I do things the way I do. But I have realised that an explanation is not always required, that the fruit of my journey will speak louder than me ever trying to justify my choice of lifestyle. I believe that this type of lifestyle will become more of the norm in the coming years as we work smarter not harder. We need to have different discussions, discussions that empower those that don't understand in new ways of living. Living authentically.

Ditch tradition
The world around us is moving so fast. The big companies in Australia are struggling for sales. Why? Because their business model is outdated. Transitioning to more modern ways of doing things is a massive undertaking for large companies. I see small to medium business rising up and taking a large part of that profit pie, but not only that, we are getting smarter about allowing our businesses to evolve and grow. We can change and adapt faster because we are smaller and it's only going to strengthen our bottom line. The Australian Bureau of Statistics reported 2.17 million actively trading businesses in Australia in June 2016, an increase of 2.4 per cent from June 2015, primarily driven by growth in small businesses ie. those with fewer than 20 employees. (More on this ⍰ http://bit.ly/1NoxUol)

If you don't keep moving in business, you will be left

behind. Being stuck in tradition and running with 'the way we've always done things', is one of the quickest ways to fold a business. Even in my fast paced marketing company, I need to be continually challenging what is, to see if there are smarter ways to do things. Being stuck in 'the way we've always done it' mindset, is dangerous in business. It's like saying we don't want growth, we are happy making what we're making. We need to get past the fear of the 'what if's', and focus on the 'what can be's'. To stay cutting edge, you must always be determining whether there are smarter ways to do things.

I wonder if Christian ministries and charities across the world are also following suit? I love seeing churches utilising Facebook lives, digital and audio technologies, to get their message out, create buzz around what they are doing, and build a following like we've never been able to create before. Just imagine the impact this is having on those that aren't in church? God is reaching and speaking to them, as they scroll through their Facebook feed, in the comfort of their own homes. It's time to assess how we can work smarter and achieve greater things for the Kingdom of God. There is a world that needs Jesus. People are starving, dying and losing hope. Our impact and service (Ministry) on the world around us, has never been more crucial. Let's challenge what is and find new ways to outwork this.

Creating new norms

Do you ever wonder how some people just seem to be functioning on a completely different wavelength? They appear to be able to achieve twelve hours work in eight, they appear to be able to run with anything asked of them, they are just in their element, constantly, always ready to respond and take action? They achieve more than the normal person does and seem to be always moving things forward, regardless of what's going on around them? I've spent a good portion of my life working through the good and the challenging, to the point now that I am just running at a completely different capacity. For the most part of my life thus far, there has always been something going on in the background, but I've had to learn to push through anyway. When I felt emotional pain, or things were really tough, I chose each time, to go and work on something that would better my future. I have become used to working at a new level of 'driven' and it's now the new norm. I don't even have to think about it, it's now the way I roll.

Authenticity is a way of life! The path of least resistance. Your best life.

Life is easier when everything is aligned and alignment is something we are always working at. Anything new can be challenging, tough, difficult and exhilarating all at the same time but if you remain consistent and committed, you will have created a new norm before you know it. Remember it takes twenty eight days to form a new habit. If something isn't working for you, find a different path, a different way to do things, a different direction and keep pushing through. Challenge yourself and create new expectations and goals. Before you know it, you'll be upleveling your life and business, and growth will just be a by-product.

Collaboration
One of the strategies that has helped me achieve six figures in the last few years (as a single mum of three

kids), is collaboration. Five to ten years ago, businesses were not working together as much, but these days collaboration is a buzzword. We are no longer so worried about someone running off with our IP (though it pays to be careful), we are starting to work together more to create better outcomes for all parties involved. I met a PR guy from Sydney at a mutual clients meeting and that one connection led me to working with a variety of corporate clients. Eighteen months later, I'm still working with those corporate clients and it has opened up a whole new range of opportunities.

I was initially asked to come onboard to help with some urgent email newsletters and to cover the social media for some events which has turned into ongoing work. This meant I was off to Melbourne for a week recently, to cover the social media for their international conference as well as being on hand to help generally where needed. I spent the week with the team, pulling off this major event, all while having a break from kids and normal routines.

Excellence allows you to stand out and pays off to the point where people cannot do without you. It was an incredibly massive week that I would never have ever dreamed I would be part of. It has lifted my confidence and expectation and vision of what is possible for the future. This experience has also given me clarity of the direction I want to take my business for the future.

Never pass up the chance to collaborate with another business and don't underestimate the potential of the opportunity. All businesses involved are enriched, everyone achieves their goals and the project comes off amazingly because there are two or three people with different talents and abilities working on it, instead of just one.

Why not find a few businesses that compliment what you offer and work together for a greater outcome. Get your referral partners in place and support each other. Everyone wins.

My business today

I could never have imagined in my wildest dreams, being where I am today and I still believe the best is yet to come. All the hard work, the pushing through the tough times, the time it's taken to learn and apply, the searching for creative solutions, the intentional creating of new norms, have all contributed to my six figure business that that continues to go from strength to strength. I am currently in the middle of changing structures and upscaling my business, so that I can be more authentically aligned with what I, the director of the business, need to be doing. To allow me to be even more flexible with my time and not be working so much on the repetitive aspects of the business, to focus on the things that only I can do, which will allow my business to grow even more.

I'm proud of everything I've achieved and with God on my side, my entrepreneurial journey will continue to impact those around me and help facilitate the calling God has on my life. The authentic life is worth fighting for even when it means saying 'no' at times. Intentionally living an authentic life, means we are living our best life, ministering and having an impact on those around us by the way we live, work and exist. It's not the end, it's just the beginning.

NIC HENRY JONES

Contributor Profile: Nic Henry Jones runs a successful digital marketing company based in the Adelaide Hills. She is cutting edge in approach, passionate about building businesses and is a leader in her industry, often being asked to run workshops and speak at various events. Her flexible and enthusiastic approach to life has seen her contribute to books as an author, MC various events and even pull off the odd cheese platter for teams she has been a part of.

Self Introduction: Supermum, Senior cheese-platter designer, Entrepreneur.

Website: www.marketmemarketing.com

Facebook: MMMarketing

Instagram: Marketmemarketing

Linkedin: Nicole Jones

Email: marketmemarketing@gmail.com

Food for thought

What were your passions as a child, teenager or young adult?

How do those passions align with who you are and what you do today?

What lessons have you learned and how have you changed as a result of difficult periods in your life?

If you feel unaligned or unfulfilled, what one action can you take to move forward?

Is the pursuit of perfection stopping you from putting your hand up to help, stifling your need for action or stopping you from achieving your full potential? If so, what needs to change to enable you to pursue excellence instead?

What qualifications or experience do you need to see your business succeed?

Do you feel frustrated with your work or business at the moment? Does your work or business line up with the authentic you? Do you need to upskill, change industries or get a different job that aligns more with your passions?

Are there other businesses nearby or in your industry that you can collaborate with? This might be with reciprocal advertising, setting up displays in another business's window or even sponsoring a team along with another complementary business. The possibilities are endless.

PART C

The Christian Entrepreneur

Final Thoughts

Chapter Eleven
When Things Get Tough

Being a Christian doesn't mean things won't get difficult at times. Life throws up all kinds of challenges, business can add another layer of pressure to our existence, and then there's the balancing and navigation of the highs and lows of seasons. Being a Christian doesn't take away the challenges, the storms don't disappear, but what our belief in God does, is give us the strength to stand up in the face of adversity and still declare, that "it is well with my soul".

Hard times can be defining factors in your Business, life and ministry. How we approach difficulty, can help make us, or break us, and everything in between, but if you make a decision amidst the chaos, that you will use this to grow, to build character, to learn something new, then we start to see some purpose threaded throughout the circumstance. The way we come out of a difficult situation, determines in part, the way we approach the next.

Knowing God and believing in something bigger than ourselves, can be the grounding factor in how we respond, where our hope lies, and what our focus should be. I've had some pretty hard times in my business, especially when there are external challenges, but I've also seen God come through in some incredible ways, bringing forth outcomes that have blown me away. As we come to the end of our The Christian Entrepreneur book, let's take a few minutes to talk about what to do when things get tough.

Prayer

Make prayer your first go to, and as soon as possible. Just know that God has all the finer details sorted, he's aware of your situation, your struggle, your difficulty, your needs. He also knows what he has in store for you for the future, the increase, the direction, the favour, the positioning, your calling. We don't always know what his plans for us are, we can't see what he sees, we just need to trust that he is Lord of all and has us under the shadow of his wings, standing firm in the knowledge that his ways are higher than ours.

The hard part is surrendering both the outcome of what it is we are believing for, the breakthroughs, the provisions and also the process. As Christians it's so easy to plan out in our minds, HOW God will work to bring breakthrough and we can also get caught up in what we think the outcome should be. I believe we need to submit our needs, wants and heart's desires to God, knowing his promises are 'yes' and 'amen', and then change our focus from what's in front of us, to who's in front of us! *'Seek first the kingdom of God and his righteousness and all these things will be added to you.' Matthew 6:33.* He already knows what you need before you ask. Spend time in prayer and worship seeking God for a creative solution. He is the ultimate creator, there is nothing he can't fix or provide a solution for. We need to start taking God at his word more.

Speak out
I've had some pretty major things unfold in my personal and business journey over the years, but I've realised that there is power in speaking out, in confiding in someone you trust, even if its a "please pray, I'm struggling with ..." The longer I sit on things on my own, the more anxious I get, when the Bible clearly states we are to be 'anxious for nothing' (Philippians 4:6–7). Don't waste time getting caught up in the what if's, the why's or the emotions. Bring light to the darkness and allow someone you trust to help you get grounded, so your next steps can be in the right direction. I have some key people I go to when things get tough in business (and life for that matter). They can help me take the emotion out of the struggle. We were never created to do life on our own and there is so much support for business out there these days too.

Rest
It's so easy when running a business to be constantly busy, working so hard to bring our dream to life, that we can be fatigued and overwhelmed without even realising it. When I look back on my own personal business journey, the times when I've gone off course, given up or just not pursued the things I should have, have been the times I have felt very tired. When we're tired ...

- Our prayer and worship time diminishes
- We don't put up a fight for the things we should be fighting for
- We hit overload fast and become reactionary rather than strategic
- We settle for second best because that's all we have time and energy for right now

- We automatically turn to survival mentalities rather than thriving strategies
- We stop going to church and connecting with others

There are times when I find myself not enjoying what I do, lacking motivation and enthusiasm and dreading Mondays. It's these times that I realise I am tired and need a break. When you start to resent working in your business, or feel like you aren't responding to people as empathetically as you normally would, it's time to pull those boundaries back in place, and give yourself a break. For me this quite often means shutting down the computer earlier, not working weekends or nights, and being fully present with kids, or other things I enjoy doing. Remember why you started that business, and readjust. Given the success of your business quite often sits with you alone, it's your direction, your vision, then it's important to prioritise time out for holidays and mini breaks. We aren't bound by the four weeks a year holiday pay situation when we work for ourselves. Take time out away from work, regularly.

Alignment & creating space for change
Feeling held back, stuck, frustrated, tired or just lost as to how to fix that internal uneasiness? It could just be that something no longer aligns. The times when I've said goodbye to situations that have not aligned with who I am as a person and what I believe I'm meant to be focusing on at that time, whether it be a relationship, a situation, a client, or participation in something, are the times when I've experienced the greatest growth, opportunities and increase in income. There have been times when my income has doubled after significant situations were over.

It's the times when I've unintentionally created space by

making these changes, by initiating a shift in focus, energy and capacity, that circumstances and situations have changed, and I've been able to regroup and reposition for what's next. We can't always see or understand God's plans, we can't even see what he is doing much of the time and we don't always have control over the outcome, but what we can change is our positioning, our focus and our alignment to what matters, what God wants to achieve through us and what we want to achieve personally.

So if you are feeling stressed, frustrated, anxious, not centered, or your body is showing physical signs of stress resulting in sickness, it might be time to assess what isn't aligned in your life and make the necessary changes.

Find your tribe

Community and relationships underpin everything we do. God desires relationship with us and we are called to come together in church as a community. There is so much research online these days about the importance of embracing community, embracing others and not doing life on your own. Ten years ago, we were all sticking to ourselves in business. But the business landscape has changed significantly, best seen in the rise of collaboration: businesses working with other businesses to generate a better outcome with all parties achieving their own goals in the process.

Find your tribe, a group of people that you can connect with, hang out with, share with when times get tough (or when things are amazing!). These might be Christian groups, but they don't need to be. These are people that will have your back in any season. Keep connecting with others and searching until you know you've found your tribe. I would recommend starting with your local church and actively seeking out other Christian business people who fellowship there. I love it that I can count on other people in my business circles to be there when I need them. It's not that often that I need to call on them, but there are times when I need a second opinion or some support. There may be some other Christian business owner groups you could attend. From time to time some of my business friends and I hangout at a winery and have a work day together. Gets us out of the office, enjoying some nice food and wine too. Find your tribe, support each other and watch your business and your life, bloom.

Give
Sounds like a random solution when things are hard, especially financially, but God has come through in some incredible ways for me when I've given to something outside of myself, when I've invested back into the Kingdom of God. We get so caught up in our situations, by looking at what we don't have, rather than focusing on God and his ability to provide for us. It's especially hard when banks are on your case, people are chasing you for money and clients aren't paying their invoices.

I have lost count of the amount of times I've heard Warren Buffet's statement 'the greatest transfer of wealth is…' or 'such and such will be the greatest transfer of wealth this generation sees …'. The shareables change for different industries, to promote their next big offering. There is always a new 'transfer of wealth' happening. All wealth comes from God, the creator of the universe, the all-powerful God, who is as present today as he was on day one. God can provide for you and go above and beyond all you could ever imagine.

I've made the decision to invest back into the Kingdom of God starting with my local church. Regardless of your stance on tithing and giving, our wealth comes from God, we have nothing without his provision. So giving, shifts our focus back to God, to something outside of ourselves. A kingdom mindset is not one of scarcity, trial and tribulation. We do experience these at times, but why would God give you a purpose then take away his provision? That's not the God I know, that's not the Bible I read. Things do get tough for sure and it's rarely straightforward, but giving back to him from the substance of everything we are, including our finances, is one way to shift our focus back on God and away from the difficulty.

I love the story of Solomon in 1 Kings 3 where Solomon goes to *Gibeon to sacrifice at the great high place (vs 4), and after offering a thousand burnt offerings on that altar (vs 5), the Lord appeared to Solomon in a dream by night and God said, "Ask! What shall I give you?"*. Solomon could have asked for anything at this point, but he asks for wisdom and an understanding heart to judge the people, that he may discern between good and evil. (vs 8 – 9). He was focused on something outside of himself. He was focused on God's plan for his life, the task God had given him. He had a very important role and he didn't take it lightly. The Lord was pleased with Solomon's response.

But what jumped out to me in this passage, is God's response. Vs 11: *'Then God said to him: "Because you have asked this thing, and have not asked long life for yourself, nor have asked riches for yourself, nor have asked the life of your enemies, but have asked for yourself understanding to discern justice, (vs 12) behold, I have done according to your words; see, I have given you a wise and understanding heart, so that there has not been anyone like you before you, nor shall any like you arise after you."*

(vs 13) **"And I have also given you what you have not asked: both riches and honor, so that there shall not be anyone like you among the kings all your days. (vs 14) So if you walk in my ways, to keep my statutes**

and my commandments, as your father David walked, then I will lengthen your days." Vs 15 Then Solomon awoke; and indeed it had been a dream. And he came to Jerusalem and stood before the ark of the covenant of the Lord, offered up burnt offerings, offered peace offerings, and made a feast for all his servants.

Solomon was focused on something outside of his own needs, on something higher and this pleased the Lord. What I love is that Solomon didn't ask for his own needs to be met, but God knew what he needed and took care of EVERYTHING else! Not just his immediate practical needs but riches and honor and influence and impact that no-one like him among the kings of his day was to have.

God knows what we need before we ask. I believe that we can position ourselves for breakthrough by investing in something outside of our own reality, the kingdom of God.

Remember your 'why'
In a practical sense, there is a reason why we start a business or why we work harder in our day job or careers. There is a reason why we want a better life, why we want things to shift. The 'why' behind what you do and why you do it, is so important. And while there may be a spiritual component, this quite naturally is a practical 'why'. In difficult or challenging times, this is one of the grounding factors that will help you to keep pushing through.

> 'When things get tough, when you want to give up, when you hit overload, remember why you started'

It's easy to get caught up in the tough stuff. There have been days on my journey where all I had the energy for was about one hour of emails. Other times, I am pumping out development projects like there's no tomorrow. My why, was and still is, freedom. I wanted to be free to be me, to work for myself, when and how I wanted to work. I wanted to be emotionally, spiritually and financially free to get on with my purpose on this earth. I wanted the freedom to be authentically aligned in every way. I don't want to just survive, I want to thrive. When chaos is imminent or difficult times arise, I focus on that one word: freedom. I may need to re-adjust my sails, make changes, learn lessons, shift my mindset and seek God, but my why is the motivation to keep going, to keep building, to keep learning. Living an authentic life in line with what God created me to be and the impact God destined me to have, has given me ultimate freedom and on the right terms. The balancing act will always be there but focus is the key.

One word

The last few years I've been choosing a word for each year. It's just been one word that connected with me at that time in my life, in whatever season I was in, one word that would help me to move forward in a certain direction, a word that would inspire me and help me to grow. It's so easy to get overwhelmed with everything we need to work on and move through, but that one word is a grounding factor in my existence and success for that year.

In 2016 I had come out of a difficult period in my life. I really didn't feel strong and confident. I came out of a situation that was not authentically aligned with who I was as a person. I was trying to find my direction again and feeling quite anxious as I embraced a new season in my life. I chose the word 'centered' as I really needed to feel grounded, centered on God and centered in the plans and purposes God had for me, even when I wasn't really seeing or feeling it. By the end of that year, I was definitely feeling 'centered'!

2017, I was feeling centered and grounded, so my word for the year was 'fierce'. Not arrogant, fierce. I wanted to be fierce in how I approached life, with some of the previous challenges having been dealt with and buried. I wanted to thrive not just survive. I wanted to love fiercely, work fiercely and go after the things I wanted in my business. I wanted to live life on the edge, to fiercely embrace all that was ahead of me. And it's been amazing to look back and see how 'fierce' and embracing this year has really been. My mind has been blown away on so many fronts.

If you were define where you want to be as a person in the coming year, your business, your success, your family, your church, in one word, what would it be?

Worship
I've chosen many times to leave the television and radio off and put on my favourite worship music. Many songs carry powerful words and it's a great way to shift our focus from what's in front of us, to who's in front of us. Whether you sing hymns on a Sunday at church or contemporary worship songs from the likes of Hillsong or Elevation church (just a few examples), let the words of those songs speak to you, encourage you and shift things in your mind, your soul and your spirit. Changing the music we play in our homes can change the atmosphere and help us move from where we are to where we need to be. Worship can take on many expressions and while there are varying definitions of worship, I think the Webster's Dictionary definition is a stand out ...

> **'Worship is to honor with extravagant love and extreme submission'.**
> **(Webster's Dictionary, 1828)**

Worship is a great way to refocus and we can use the words of songs in our prayers too, especially in those times of being unsure of what to pray. Many of the hymns that have been sung for years started out as prayers from someone's heart and the words are powerful and uplifting.

Worship moves your focus from what's in front of you, to who's in front of you.

Worship allows you to stand firm when things are crumbling around you and still honestly declare from deep within that 'it is well with your soul'.

Worship declares God's power, goodness, grace, mercy and love, changing your stance from unsure to sure.

Worship centres you, regardless of what's happening externally.

Worship moves us out of the way and allows God to do his work.

Worship is surrender to his ways and letting go of our ways.

In His Name and for His Glory ...

NIC HENRY JONES

Our Authors

Amy Revell is an author, podcaster, blogger and professional organiser. Amy has always been a super organised person, and this natural gift has developed into a successful business helping women find freedom through decluttering and organising their homes.

The Declutter Queen and minimalist who loves an organising project and drinking tea with friends.

Website: www.simplyorganised.net
Facebook: simplyorganisedPO
Linkedin: Amy Revell
Instagram: simply.organised
Email: amy.revell@simplyorganised.net

Maree Cutler-Naroba is a multi-skilled Business Strategist and Educator, Digital Content Writer and Child Protection Practitioner/Lawyer, who is also affectionately known as The Ideas Guru. She uses a range of styles and methods to provide information, insights and ideas to management, staff, students and clients that is relevant, practical, creative and timely.

God-lover on a mission to help as many women as I can give wings to their business and career dreams AND a passionate advocate for the protection of children from abuse and neglect.

Websites: www.mareecutlernaroba.com
www.boomersbizgym.com
Facebook: ideas2propelu
Linkedin: Maree Cutler Naroba
Instagram: maree_cutler_naroba
Email: mcnaroba@gmail.com

Our Authors

Nic Henry Jones runs a successful digital marketing company based in the Adelaide Hills. She is cutting edge in approach, passionate about building business, and is a leader in her Industry, often getting asked to run workshops and speak at various events. Her flexible and enthusiastic approach to life has seen her contribute to books as an Author, MC various events, and even pull off the odd cheese platter and event for teams she is a part of.

Supermum, Senior Cheese-platter Designer, Entrepreneur.
Website: www.marketmemarketing.com
Facebook: MMMarketing
Instagram: Marketmemarketing
Linkedin: Nicole Jones
Email: marketmemarketing@gmail.com

Linda Chaousis wears a lot of hats. A writer. A speaker. A podcaster. A wellness advocate. And yet, every one of these has a common passionate thread of hers going through-to encourage others to follow their path even if others say 'why would you do that?'.

Her favourite place is any beach at times with her dogs and a good hot latte. Oh yeah!

Website: www.lindachaousis.com
Facebook: thinkitbelieveitcreateit
Linkedin: Linda Chaousis
Email: linda@lindachaousis.com

Our Authors

David Daddow has been involved in the Self Storage industry for 30 years, seeing the highs and lows of business expansion to now include multiple locations. He is an Industry leader, serving on an Australasian Board, and also project managing house builds in Fiji with C3.

An entrepreneur at heart, he's a quiet but highly respected achiever, and loves living in the Adelaide Hills.

Website: https://ableselfstorage.com.au/
Facebook: david.daddow.1
Linkedin: David Daddow
Email: selfstoragesa@gmail.com

Peter Horsfield asks what is the one thing that changes everything? It is common to every single individual, relationship, family, team, company, economy, country and nation. The one thing that if removed will destroy the most powerful government, successful business, greatest friendship and the deepest love. On the other hand if developed and leveraged, this one thing has the potential to create unparalleled success and prosperity in every dimension life has to offer. This one thing is Trust.

Coffee addicted lover of life who lives and breathes epic digital marketing strategies. Living the dream!

Website: www.peterhorsfield.com.au
Facebook: peterhorsfieldcfp
Linkedin: Peter Horsfield
Email: peterhorsfieldcfp@gmail.com

Our Authors

Darryl Stringer has been an architectural and real estate photographer since 1998. With a lot of persistence he built a very successful business, and he's now available to share that knowledge on marketing, pricing and photography with others, making their journey as a photographer a little bit easier. **A quiet achiever who loves sport, dark chocolate, and thinking outside the box.**

Website: www.BuildAPhotographyBusiness.com
Facebook: realestatephotographysystem
Linkedin: Darryl Stringer
Email: darryl@realestatephotographysystem.com

Brenda Tsiaousis inspires confidence and ignites courage while helping entrepreneurs globally realise their full potential in life, business and entrepreneurship. She provides a powerful blend of business and life coaching with a core message of the importance of developing "The Courage To Bloom" to a growing community of women in Australia and around the world. She is a Business Potentialist, Author and Speaker, and a highly regarded leader in her field.

Prolific speaker, green tea lover and proud mum to 4 beautiful children, and wife to her gorgeous Greek husband!

Website: www.brendatsiaousis.com
Facebook: BrendaTsiaousis
Linkedin: Brenda Tsiaousis
Email: BrendaTs@BrendaTsiaousis.com

Our Authors

Charmayne Chinnery is the CEO at Essential Grace, a business specialising in the use of essential oils for better health and well being. She is passionate about helping people renew mindsets and well being so they can be the best version of themselves.

Passionate, empowered and making an impact.

Facebook: essentialgrace1
Email: charmayne.essentialgrace@gmail.com

You must decide...

IF YOU ARE GOING TO ROB THE WORLD OR BLESS IT WITH THE RICH, VALUABLE, POTENT, UNTAPPED RESOURCES LOCKED AWAY WITHIN YOU'.

DR. MYLES MUNROE

www.ingramcontent.com/pod-product-compliance
Lightning Source LLC
Chambersburg PA
CBHW071449080526
44587CB00014B/2047